Wild Geese Sorrow

Wild Geese Sorrow

THE CHINESE WALL INSCRIPTIONS
AT ANGEL ISLAND

Translated from the Chinese by Jeffrey Thomas Leong

CALYPSO EDITIONS

CALYPSO EDITIONS
www.CalypsoEditions.org

By unearthing literary gems from previous generations, translating foreign writers into English with integrity, and providing a space for talented new voices, Calypso Editions is committed to publishing books that will endure in both content and form. Our only criterion is excellence.

Cover photo/illustration: Elizabeth West
Interior photos: Jeffrey Thomas Leong; Architectural Resources Group; Angel Island State Park, State of California; National Archives
Author photo: Sam Willard Photography
INS Interrogation: PaperSon.com/Byron Yee

The anonymous Chinese poems were first discovered on the Angel Island barracks walls and are in the public domain.
Translations and text © Jeffrey Thomas Leong
Copyright © 2018 Calypso Editions
Printed in the United States of America
First Edition

ISBN 13: 978-1-944593-06-3

TABLE OF CONTENTS

FOREWORD

To reach San Francisco from Hong Kong you have traveled nearly seven thousand miles, on a steamer journey of more than three weeks; the conditions on the ship have been brutal and cramped. The year might be 1910 or 1925 or 1938. Because of the Chinese Exclusion Act of 1882, you will only be allowed to enter the United States if you can prove that one of your relatives is lawfully living in what you hope will be your new homeland. And when you at last reach your destination, you find yourself incarcerated in a rude wooden barracks at the Angel Island Immigration Station, with scores of other hopeful Chinese immigrants, most of them like you, men in their early twenties.

You are aware that the American authorities will question you in order to determine that you are indeed who you claim to be. Before leaving, you were told to expect the interrogators' questions to be pedantic, relentless, and exhausting. Their goal is to trip you up, catch you in a falsehood. Until proven otherwise, you are assumed to be a "paper son," who has fabricated the identities of your relatives. You have prepared for this onslaught, memorizing every possible detail about your family history, your village and its inhabitants. You have in essence had to create through memorization, a kind of personal Wikipedia or Google Earth.

After days, weeks, or months of detention, your interrogation at last takes place. You sit at a table before two questioners and a stenographer. You were wise to prepare for this moment so studiously. The questions are just as unrelenting as you were told. They are bellicose, dehumanizing, and in places downright surreal.

*

Here is a portion of the interrogation of a detainee named Yee Bing Quai:

Q. When did your alleged father come to the United States?

A. I do not know. He came before I was born.

Q. Has your alleged father made any trips to China since he came to the U.S.?

A. I have never seen my father—my mother told me he returned to the U.S. in CR 14.

Q. If you have never seen your alleged father, how do you recognize the photograph attached to the affidavit you present, as being that of your alleged father?

A. YEE MON TOY of the JEW THIN NGIN store, Bonham Strand, Hong Kong, gave me the affidavit when I went to Hong Kong on my way to the U.S.; and he told me that that was a picture of my father.

Q. Did you ever see any photograph of your alleged father prior to the time you saw the photograph attached to the affidavit?

A. Yes, there is a bust photograph of my father, dressed in American clothes, enclosed in a frame with a glass front, about 6 x 8 inches, which is hanging on the back wall of the center room of my house in HIN village, HPD, China. That photograph of my father has been hanging there as long as I can remember. My mother told me that it was a picture of my father that he sent to her a long time ago. She did not say when he sent her the picture.

The interrogators' queries are horrific for many reasons, one of them being their guileless debasement of the functions and purposes of language. At its best, the vocabulary of jurisprudence can be exacting, elegant, and even poetic: Kafka's storied prose style derives in no small measure from his years of writing legal briefs. At its worst, the lingo of jurisprudence is a blunt-force ideological weapon, using what is ostensibly a desire for precision and truth-telling to give falsehood and injustice a veneer of legal respectability. During the Great Terror of the late 1930s, Stalin's secret police coerced hundreds of thousands of false confessions from his victims; many of them are jaw-droppingly detailed and sadly ingenious in their fabrications of Crimes Against The State.

We see a similar perverse ingeniousness in the Angel Island interrogators' methods as they are evidenced in the passage above—the coldly calculated repetitions of "alleged father" are surely the most striking example. Of course, the detainees at Angel Island were probably not thinking of the niceties of linguistics and ideology during their interrogations: they simply wanted to begin new lives in the United States.

And yet it is also clear that, before and after their interrogations, many of the Angel Island detainees were indeed thinking of matters of linguistics and ideology, and of how the making of art can serve to redeem words when their uses have been sullied. The Rumanian-born poet Paul Celan was fluent in several languages. In his Bremen address—perhaps the most acute encapsulation of his aesthetic—Celan explained why he chose to write in German, the language of those who sent his sister and parents to the death camps. His purpose, he said, was the cleanse and re-sanctify of the German tongue, to once again make poetry from a language that the Third Reich had made into an instrument of what he called "death-bringing speech."

No matter what language one employs, to write poetry is always to indict those who would turn our words into death-bringing speech. The poems written by the Angel Island detainees are an especially noteworthy and poignant example of such an indictment. Over two hundred of them have survived: each one is a blow to the Big Lie and to linguistic degradation.

*

Imagine the scene: it is nearing dawn, and you have spent a sleepless night in your Angel Island barrack, awaiting tomorrow's interrogation. Your thoughts turn homeward, and they turn to the forms and sensibilities of the Classical Chinese poetry which you studied and memorized in school. And now, carrying a contraband candle and pen-knife, while your fellow detainees snore in their bunks, you offer up your own poem. You do not write the poem, you *incise* it into the soft wood of the barracks wall, knowing full well that your captors will destroy it as soon as it is discovered. You do not even sign your name to your creation. And the poem may look something like this:

Deep Night

In the still of the night, small sounds are a howling wind.
Shadows, an ache of old wounds, so I recite verse:
Fog and mist drift, a gloomy sky,
Insects rub crick-crack beneath the moon's frail light,
My sad bitter face matches these heavens.
A worried man sits alone, leans at the window's sill.
                                    — Toishan (formerly known as Yee)

Or, not surprisingly, your poem might conclude with something less wistful:

Come that day when China unites,
I myself will rip out the barbarian's heart and guts.

Or, instead of resolve and anger, the tone of your poem—again, not surprisingly—might end in abjection and anguish:

At mid-ship, I'll suffer waves, and pearl-like tears will fall.
On a clear night, three times I'll find the bitterness hard to bear.

*

The story of the near-miraculous survival of the Angel Island wall poems has now been often-told, and images of the poems are widely available on the internet. Various English translations of the poetry exist, although a fair percentage of them seem to eschew the poems' literary merit, emphasizing instead their sociological or historical significance. This emphasis is not surprising, but it can have the unintended effect of presenting the poems as a kind of graffiti rather than as artistic efforts, many of them impressive by any writerly standard.

Jeffrey Thomas Leong is himself a fine poet, and his translations of 70 of the poems are nuanced, affecting, and informed by a haunting but astringent music. They do commendable justice to the Angel Island poets, writers who were not welcomed to these shores—but who nevertheless made a crucial and indelible contribution to our national literary culture.

–David Wojahn, 2017

INTRODUCTION

Once I sat with my parents and sister at the nightly dinner table, and my father told us of his return trip to the United States with his village cousin and their subsequent interrogations at Angel Island. My father's papers identified him as the son of a native son, and he passed easily, whereas his cousin, purported to be my father's brother, did not and was eventually deported back to China. Though this "failure" by his cousin was not my father's doing, it haunted him the rest of his life.

My father also recounted traveling by ship to San Francisco with my grandfather, when at a winter stop in Shanghai, a white sailor tossed a pail of dirty galley water below onto a Chinese sampan family selling *jook*. Livid and in imitation, my father flailed his arms about describing how my grandfather used his martial arts skills to slam the bucket upon the sailor's head. On the other hand, my mother immigrated from China at the tender age of nine months, so preliterate and pre-memory, had no details to give about her journey.

Thus like my father, my earliest memories of Angel Island began in the same tone of anger, shame and regret shared by many of the 160,000 or so Chinese immigrants processed through the immigration facility. I knew not much more, after graduating in 1970 with a degree in Asian American Studies from the University of California, Berkeley, where I participated in the Third World Liberation Front strike, an effort led by students of color to teach our suppressed history of discrimination and led to the founding of Berkeley's Ethnic Studies Department. There I took classes in order to relearn conversational Cantonese, a language I had once spoken as a child.

Some years later, the ground-breaking book, *Island: Poetry and History of Chinese Immigrants on Angel Island 1910-1940* appeared, authored by fellow community activists; it included translations of about 135 Chinese wall poems from the Angel Island Immigration Station. For a long while I did not appreciate the significance of this work as I raised a family and spent my working career providing health care to the poor through San Francisco's public health system. But upon retiring, I reignited my passion for writing and received an MFA in poetry from the Vermont College of Fine Arts. While in graduate school, I rediscovered these poems at an Angel Island Immigration Station open house.

With the goal of preservation, the Angel Island Immigration Station buildings and grounds have been designated a National Historic Site after years of advocacy with State and Federal agencies. The men's barracks have been restored, and work is now being done on the former hospital building. Inspired by my daughter, I discovered I was able to translate the Angel Island poems into English using a combination of bilingual skills and secondary internet resources. With assistance from faculty advisers and after several years of effort, I've been able to produce the translations herein presented.

Significance of the Angel Island Wall Poetry

Choosing to employ the Tang Chinese poetic tradition brought with them to America, the Angel Island detainees expressed their deepest feelings of anger, resentment and political outrage in rhyme and verse. Written *in situ*, these poems are a cross between Anna Swir's chronicling of the Warsaw Uprising of 1944 in her book *Building the Barricades*, and the poems of Miklos Radnoti, which were plucked from his jacket pocket when his body was exhumed from a World War II mass grave. It is a poetry of resistance, or as often-called, the "poetry of witness," which documents the unbearable hardships suffered by human beings. But I would venture to say the Angel Island work is also a poetry of resilience, persistence and perseverance, and eventually of the spirit's prevail.

Why was there an Angel Island Immigration Station in the first place? Historically, the Chinese Exclusion Act of 1882 was the first U.S. immigration law passed to target a specific ethnic group, and it severely restricted Chinese immigration to scholars, businessmen, and a few other groups. In 1906 the Great Earthquake and Fire destroyed San Francisco's City Hall and concurrently all birth records, so any person could claim that he or she was a native-born citizen. Thus post-earthquake, if an aspiring immigrant could demonstrate a U.S. birth, or prove status as the child of a native-born American, he or she could successfully immigrate.

Absent valid birth documentation in the U.S. and China, proof of eligible immigration status was based solely upon oral testimony and witness corroboration. This system of personal declaration created much room for misrepresentation which, from the Chinese immigrant point of view, became a method to circumvent racist and unfair U.S. immigration laws. In response, in 1910 U.S. immigration officials created the Angel Island Immigration Station for the express purpose of screening false claims to immigrate and enforce the exclusionary provisions of existing laws. When the immigration station closed in 1940, and after the processing of denials and successful appeals, records show that only about 5% of detainees were deported back to China.

From the Immigration Station's inception, wall poems began to appear expressing detainee anger and frustration. Poems were at first ink-brushed, but when painted over by officials, detainees took to carving them into the Douglas Fir-planked walls. The official response was to putty the inscriptions, ironically serving to preserve them for the ages. This literary "cat and mouse" game continued throughout all the Immigration Station's history.

The Angel Island poetry is significant as an early use of traditional Chinese literary forms with content wholly about an American experience, and is arguably the first Chinese American literary text, albeit published on walls, by persons literally fresh off the boat and caught in their first moments of becoming American. Yunte Huang, a professor of Asian American Studies at the University of California, Santa Barbara, has written that the Angel Island poems are too a form of traditional Chinese tibishi wall poetry (題壁詩), a subgenre of Chinese travel poetry, where compositions are placed in public spaces for general consideration. Such work, frequently historical in nature and subversive to officially-sanctioned narratives, might appear on walls, at city gates and mountain inns, and were often carved in beautiful calligraphy into wood, stone or other materials.

At Angel Island, the detainees wrote of their immediate experiences: journeying from China, daily life, worries about interrogation and finances, family affairs back home, health exams, fears of deportation, transnational politics, and survival strategies. Critical analyses of the Angel Island immigration experience have been presented recently from personal essays to scholarly studies, and oral histories from former detainees have been wisely recorded. But the wall poems are unique. They express in a direct manner the deep feelings of the detainees through imagery and a creative aesthetic, capturing the detainee's fears, worries, grief and anger, thus holding a power not found in other sources.

One example is in a poem describing the journey by ship from Guangdong province to San Francisco, California which often took two to three weeks. Life on board consisted of seasickness or studying from crib books in preparation for the anticipated interrogations at Angel Island. Fellow passengers from the native village would assist one another in coaching to memory the minute details of assumed personas, including the number of steps at a house's front door or the location of the family's clock. At mid-journey, near Honolulu, these cheat sheets were tossed into the Pacific to avoid detection by immigration officials.

In this poem, the journey is described using vivid imagery, e.g. "I ate wind and tasted sea for more than twenty days" (Poem 7) Additional impressions include "heavy seas," "wind and frost," "bought an oar," and "huge waves." In the tradition of Tang poetry, image is juxtaposed in a paratactical manner to create a contrasted landscape of understated emotion.

Writing and Carving the Poems

For this collection, I have chosen 70 of the more than 200 identified poems and poem fragments from the Angel Island Immigration Station. The poems were selected to provide a cross-section of experience and sentiment over the 30 year life of the site presented in a more or less chronological manner. Care was taken to avoid redundancies, whether in subject matter, style or tone, particularly in regards to the traditional use of historical and literary allusions, which are difficult to translate successfully. Tang poetry is extremely elastic in subject matter despite its strict conventions of form, holding themes as disparate as an out-of-sorts scholar drunkenly lamenting his fate, veiled critiques of dynastic founders, and ethereal Zen Buddhist appreciations of absence and presence. Some of that suppleness is evident too in the subject matter of the Angel Island poems.

Some question the literary value of this work. Academic scholars used to the literary refinements of Du Fu or Li Bai may not find that same level of craft in this work. Some Chinese American descendants of Angel Island detainees may feel "embarrassed" at the perceived sophomoric attempts by their ancestors, within an overall context of cultural inferiority of their own "Chinese-ness." And then, there is the shame of the Angel Island experience itself. Attitudes of which I would say would be wrong-minded.

To seriously address literary legitimacy, it is critical to understand who the Angel Island poets were and of their writing process. Of the surviving poems, all were either found on the men's barracks walls, in the so-called *muhk nguk* or "wood house," or were purported to be copied from these walls sometime during the course of the thirty year life of the Immigration Station. The first poems were seen and noticed within a month of Angel Island's opening, and were originally written (brush-stroked) in ink on the barrack walls.

Virtually all the poems were unsigned, which is understandable considering that the poets were also prospective immigrants awaiting approval of their petitions and wanting to avoid identification as political "rabble rousers." Poems were too mostly untitled, not necessarily common in Chinese poetry, but perhaps more of a practical function of quickly carving characters surreptitiously into precious wall space. Lastly, the poems were not dated with a few exceptions.

But it is easily apparent from the different tones, diction, syntax and subject matter of this work that there were many distinct "voices," and hence presumably, authors, though we virtually have no personal information about any, except a few like Smiley Jann, a former detainee and one of two early compilers of the wall poetry. Jann included a poem he wrote in his Angel Island poetry anthology; whether that poem was written during or after his detention is unknown.

What we do know is some basic demographic information on the 160,000 Chinese immigrants who passed through Angel Island, mostly male and from the towns and villages in Guangdong province, in the Sei Yahp, Zhongshan, and other districts around Guangzhou. We know that these predominately working class men, sons of farmers, merchants, etc.

had varying degrees of education, from small village schools and private tutoring. Chinese education during this time period was based on rote memorization, and the language arts (see Translator's Notes) was often taught using Confucian classics and other texts which were written in poetic forms.

The Chinese written language is quite different from the multitudinous spoken dialects of Chinese, yet it was universally taught and therefore widely understood. In the primary and secondary education of Chinese, mostly young men (patriarchal China rarely educated young women) learned to read, recite, and compose poetry. The practice of reading and composing poetry was core to the learned, scholarly tradition and even remained a part of civil service examinations through 1911. Mao Tsetung, one of modern China's most famous warrior-scholars, was an accomplished composer of classical Chinese poetry.

Thus it was not surprising that consistent with Chinese poetic tradition, young male Angel Island detainees took to expressing their anguish and disgust by carving poetry into the walls of the men's barracks for fellow compatriots to read. These carvings were a free and instant form of publishing, not unlike the blogs and tweets of our own historical period. It should be noted that poetry was also seen in the women's second floor quarters in the Administration building, which unfortunately was destroyed by fire in 1940. To date, no records or copies of individual poems written by women poets are known to exist.

Yet one should not overstate nor romanticize the influence of the Angel Island poets in their day, for it's just as likely that many fellow detainees ignored the wall writings as read them. Many were teenagers or children uninterested in adult angst. It's likely that the authors were longer term, older detainees with lengthy bouts of boredom to kill. And perhaps like today, not everyone liked or read poetry. But these poems have survived to express eloquently a particularly intense period in Chinese American experience. It's not known whether any Angel Island poets continued to write after having left the Immigration Station, though scholars like Marlon Hom have identified poetry writing circles in the world of San Francisco's Chinatown.

Of particular interest are strong images repeated and expressed in the Angel Island poems: that of the orphan body, Terrace for Gazing

Homeward, the Jing Wei bird, and wild geese sorrow. On the one hand there was a language of grief, displacement and oppression previously existent in Chinese literature for detainees to utilize in stating their innermost thoughts and feelings, a small consolation. But possibly more difficult for us to understand as Americans with a mere 250-year collective history, is the comfort received by detainees in placing their trials within a literary context of a 4,000 year old civilization. To say that they were like Ruan Ji is on the one level to inspire heroic feelings, but on another, to believe that they were in fact questing heroes, in their very first days and weeks on American soil.

A few words should be added about the physical space at the Angel Island Immigration Station men's barracks. Poems are located on every possible square inch of the walls and have been preserved to protect against further deterioration. However, the poems remain largely painted over, puttied in various stages of uncover and reveal. The text as artifact exists in a somewhat damaged state and partially in fragments. Detainees carved poems from their top-tier bunk beds onto the highest sections of the walls, though eye-level areas were the most desirable. As a designated national historic site, the space is subject to strict rules for restoration which both hamper discovery efforts as well as guarantee a basic preservation. I believe that the physical site warrants further investigation and study.

Translator's Note

Much has been written about the difficulties of translating from the character-based, visual semiotics of the Chinese language to the text-based, alphabet-driven symbols of English. Professor Wai-Lim Yip, the Taiwanese poet and translator, compares it to the difference between the original Apple and Window-based computer operating systems though a notable convergence in graphic interfaces has occurred. Many of the key Tang poetry characteristics, such as tonal parallelism and end-rhyme are either impossible to translate or would produce an English equivalent that is wooden or bizarrely 19th century and incomprehensible. The key word is: "equivalent."

What I've tried to do is to produce a text that is readable as an English language poem, yet remains as true as possible to its original Chinese in both form and content. For me, content has not been as problematic as form. In form, I've tried to maintain at minimum, the imagistic minimalism and parataxis that exists in the original but needed to add some filler words such as prepositions, verbs, verb tenses, etc. to produce a clear poem in the target language. I've tried also to use plain diction and to avoid American idioms if at all possible. Of greater importance is what I would call the issue of "tone."

What is "tone," in poetry? It is every craft element that can provide shades of meaning in a poem, and thus includes:

1. Diction – whether high, low or medium
2. Syntax – word order (regular grammar, elided, fragmented)
3. Sound – use of rhymes (alliteration, assonance, repetition, end-rhyme)
4. Imagery – whether popular or classical, everyday or historical allusion

For me, the overall tone of the Angel Island poems is undeniably one of anger, frustration and outrage. This angry tone uses the above elements and is expressed within classical Tang poetics and its extensive technical requirements. The following is a step-by-step illustration of how I've attempted to translate this angry tone for a 21st century reader. The example is from Poem 4 of this collection.

Poem 4

1. 黃家子弟本香城,
2. 挺身投筆赴美京.
3. 買棹到了金山地,
4. 誰知撥我過埃崙.
5. 我國圖強無此樣,
6. 船泊岸邊直可登.

7. 民國十三廿肆晨
8. 逍遙子鐵城閒筆

Here is the original eight-line Chinese text in its modern layout, to be read from left to right, then top down. (Lines 7 and 8 are the signature of the poet, and not part of the poem's meaning per se.) It should be noted that the original Chinese text presented elsewhere in this collection is in its traditional layout, reading top down, then right to left, which is the same layout used in the original men's barracks carvings. I've used the original format to give a visual sense of the work as physical artifact.

Then, I made the following transliteration (romanization) into Yale Cantonese using Internet resources. (A Mandarin Pinyin transliteration was also made.)

1. Wòhng	gà	jái	daih	bún	Hèung	Sèhng
2. Ting	sàn	tauh	bāt	fuh	Méih	jīng
3. Máaih	zaauh	dou	liuh	Gām	Sàan	deih
4. Séuih	jì	buht	ngóh	gwo	āi	lún
5. Ngóh	gwok	tòuh	kéuhng	mòuh	chí	yéung
6. Syùhn	bohk	ngohn	bīn	jihk	hak	dang
7. Mahn	gwok	sahp	sahm	yah	sei	sahn
8. Sui	waih	jái	tit	sèhng	hàahn	bāt

This eight line Tang style poem uses slant end-rhymes. Within its traditional seven character line, it groups characters into images and juxtaposes these, to create leaps of meaning. Further juxtaposition is used between couplet lines to pair contrasting ideas.

Next, a word-for-word translation is made from Internet resources.

1. Huang	family	son	younger brother	this	Fragrant	City
2. Straighten	body	cast	writing brush	go	America	capitol
3. Buy	oar	to	the	Gold	Mountain	ground
4. Who	knew	assign	I	cross	Island	-
5. My	country	map chart	strength	no	this kind	of way
6. Boat	anchor	shore	edge	straight	away	ascend
7. Nationalist	China	13th year	-	twenty	four	morning
8. Leisurely	thoroughfare	child	Iron	City	idle	writing brush, pen

This "raw" translation gives a sense of the poem's meaning in very general terms.

I then made my English literary translation based upon the word-for-word with the following result:

> I, young son of the Wong clan from Hèung Sèhng,
> straightened up, tossed my writing brush,
>   to quest for America's capitol.
> I bought an oar, came to the place of Gold Mountain.
> Who knew I would be sent to this Island?
> If my country were strong, it would not be like this.
> When the ship docks, up a gangway straight to shore.

> *Written at dawn,*
> *24th day in the 13th Year of the Republic,*
> *the idle pen of a lazy boy from the City of Iron.*

In this translation, I've tried to maintain the line length, syntax, juxtaposition and imagery within the original. This translation does foreground the implicit "I," typical first person speaker of Tang poetry, but uses plainspoken medium level diction without slang. It tries to balance the form and content (i.e. structure and meaning) of the original.

In general, I've employed additional guidelines for the Angel Island poem forms. For 4-line quatrains, many are kept in their original lineated format, but others are broken into shorter lines. In breaking the traditional Tang Chinese line, I aim for its middle, consistent with the typical pattern of 1-2, 3-4, and 5-6-7 character units, so that the English language lines are parsed in complete units of meaning, more similar to the Chinese. I have chosen not to enjamb across meaning units as in a more free verse style of translation, which may make for a slightly more interesting English language poem, but arguably would be a disservice to the Chinese original. For most longer 8-line poems, I've left the Chinese line format intact, but have presented the poem as a double quatrain with a stanza break after the fourth line, unless meaning calls for one stanza only. For poems with more than 8 lines, I've broken them into stanzas in a manner to further the poem's meaning. As can be seen, formatting of the English translation is more of an art than a science.

It should be noted that one of the great challenges as well as pleasures of translating Chinese poetry are the many meanings given to the same word depending upon its location next to other words, its "neighborhood" or context. This arranging creates a vast word puzzle to solve, but at the same time allows for flexibility in divining sense. Because of the great variances that can occur in interpreting meaning in a Chinese poem, no single translation can be guaranteed to please all.

Summary

The Angel Island Immigration Station was historically created to exclude Chinese immigrants by virtue of their race and nationality. Yet once that strategy was abandoned when China became a U.S. ally during World War II, the past was forgotten as if that chapter of American history had never happened. It was only through the efforts of Chinese immigrant descendants that a painful birthright, the poetry upon the walls of the men's barracks, has been preserved, not only out of pride for what our forebears suffered and overcame but also to serve as a constant reminder of the difficulties other immigrants, refugees and stateless people experience today.

But what purpose did these wall poems serve to their original authors? Given the basic education received by these new immigrants, their act of writing poetry was transformational; by taking hardship and expressing it artistically, they elevated it to the archetypal. An expression of personal feeling may be therapeutic in a Western sense, but for these immigrants it was also communal, literally on the walls of the barracks in which they were detained and for all their compatriots to see. It was too, in a real sense, their own contribution to the history of Chinese literature. And it can be said to American literature as well.

It is hoped that this work inspires displaced peoples everywhere to express their difficult worlds in words and verse. In the tradition of Anna Ahkmatova, Paul Celan, and Czeslaw Milosz, words may not be able to actually save lives but can make life itself worth saving. May we have the wisdom to read what is carved on those future walls.

Wild Geese Sorrow

雁

哀

I. ORIGINAL PLAN

1.

拋妻子，歷盡重洋受幾多風霜，不知袛為家貧求白璧；

別親朋，萬里飄流，難計捱一切雨雪，都緣囊澀重青蚨。

1.

Leaving behind wife and child,
      I've experienced heavy seas.
Don't know how much wind and frost I've endured.
Because my family was poor, I sought the precious
      white jade.

Separated from relatives and friends,
      I drifted about, 10,000 *li*.
It's difficult to calculate suffering in one slice
      of rain and snow,
All due to a purse empty of weighty green coin.

2.

美洲金銀實可愛，
錐股求榮動程來。
不第千金曾用盡，
犁黑面目為家哉。

2.

American silver and gold are my true obsessions.
Jabbing an awl into my thigh to seek glory,
        I've journeyed here.
But a thousand precious coins already spent,
I've plowed the fields until my face blackened.
        All for family!

3.

凡我國之人；
因謂家分起。
賣田又賣地；
欲往來花旗。
家人向住汝；
誰知難上難。

3.

Whereas, my countryman, the family was split up to advance
Selling off fields and acres wanting at least one to arrive
        in the Land of the Flower Flag,
Support of the relatives now rests with you.
Who can even know this hardship upon hardships!

4.

黃家子弟本香城，
挺身投筆赴美京，
買棹到了金山地，
誰知撥我過埃崙。
我國圖强無此樣，
船泊岸邊直可登。
民國十三廿肆晨，
逍遙子鐵城閒筆。

4.

I, young son of the Wong clan from Hèung Sèhng,
straightened up, tossed my writing brush,
     to quest for America's capitol.
I bought an oar, came to the place of Gold Mountain.
Who knew I would be sent to this island?
If my country were strong, it would not be like this.
When the ship docked, up a gangway straight to shore.

Written at dawn,
24th day in the 13th Year of the Republic,
the idle pen of a lazy boy from the City of Iron.

5.

離時父母恨忽忽；
飲怨長漣奔海外。
欲免命舛困囚中；
誰教國族悲時切？
侵凌親恩抱罪隆；
未報鳴蟲哀冷夜。
今也幽咽苦喉嚨；
不單。

鄭文舫題

5.

When I left, my parents regretted the hurry,
I drank my resentment tear by tear because of poverty.
Wanting to avoid endless hunger, I fled overseas,
Who teaches me life's irony, trapped inside a prison?

Bullied and invaded, a nation's people mourn sad times,
To have not repaid my parent's kindness bears
        tremendous guilt.
Presently, a cry of worms, chilled night,
Not only do I sob alone but bitterness fills my throat.

Smiley Jann

6.

阻攔上埠實堪憐，
撥回歸家也心驚。
無面見江東父老，
只望求富反求貧。

6.

Barred from landing at the port, I truly should be pitied.
To be pushed to return home makes my heart tremble.
Meeting the elders again east of the river would be a loss of face.
I came seeking wealth, but instead reaped poverty.

7.

本擬舊歲來美洲，
洋蚨迫阻到初秋。
織女會牛郎哥日，
乃搭林肯總統舟，
餐風嘗浪廿餘日，
幸得平安抵美洲。
以為數日可上埠，
點知苦困木樓囚。
番奴苛待真難受，
感觸家境淚雙流。
但願早登三藩市，
免在此間倍添愁。

7.

Last year, my original plan: to come to America,
But lack of money for passage stopped me
        until early autumn.
On the Seventh Day of the Seventh Moon,
I boarded the *President Lincoln.*
I ate sea wind and tasted waves for more than twenty days,
But luckily, arrived unharmed.
I thought a few days and I'd be on the dock,
Little did I know of the suffering in the wood house.
The barbarians' harsh treatment really difficult to accept,
Thinking of my family finances, a double stream of tears.
Yet, I hope to enter San Francisco soon,
Avoid living in this limbo which lengthens all worry.

8.

為乜來由要坐監？
祗緣國弱與家貧。
椿萱倚門無消息，
妻兒擁被歎孤單。
縱然批准能上埠，
何日滿載返唐山？
自古出門多變賤。
從來征戰幾人還？

8.

For what reason must I sit in jail?
It's because my country's weak and the family poor.
My parents lean at the door, but there's no news.
My wife and son squeeze beneath a quilt,
      sigh like lonely orphans.

Even if I were permitted to rise up the gangway,
When would I have a full load to return to Tang Mountain?
Since ancient times, leaving home results
      in worthless change.
From expeditions, how many men ever return?

9.

國民不為甘為牛，
意至美洲作營謀。
洋樓高聳無緣住，
誰知樓所是監牢？

9.

A nation's citizen unwilling to be a complacent ox,
My intent, come to America to make a living.
Foreign houses may be lofty and grand,
    but I've no reason to live in them.
Yet, who knew the place I stay would be
    a locked jail?

10.

木屋間來把窗開，
曉風明月共徘徊。
故鄉遠憶雲山斷，
小島微聞寒雁哀。
失路英雄空說劍，
窮途騷士且登台。
應知國弱人心死，
何事囚困此處來？

10.

Bored in the wood house I held open a window,
Dawn breezes, the day-bright moon, linger together.
In distant memory, an old village, hills obscured by clouds,
On this small island, tiny cries of wild geese sorrow.

The mighty hero who's lost his way speaks emptily of the sword,
A troubled scholar on a poor road writes only high poems.
You should know when a country is weak,
     the people's spirit dies.
How else have we come to be trapped here as prisoners?

II. DETAINED IN THE WOOD HOUSE

Poem 23

11.

埃崙此地為仙島，
山野原來是監牢。
既望張網焉投入？
祗為囊空莫奈何。

11.

Angel Island is the "island of immortals,"
Yet the hills and fields I've come to are in fact a prison.
I saw the open net, so why did I throw myself in?
Because of an empty wallet, I had no other choice.

came here to get money
and a better life. It is a
prision not what they
expected

12.

家徒壁立始奔波，
浪聲歡同笑呵呵。
埃崙念到聞禁往，
無非皺額奈天何。

12.

Family members jumped up, began to rush about.
A joyous breaking wave, like laughter, *Ha, ha!*
Arriving at Island, when told we couldn't land,
Everywhere, furrowed brows.
 How to endure heaven's fate?

13.

辛亥十月初五
搬房有感而作

到來木屋一星期；
提起搬房我極悲。
執齊行李忙忙走；
其中苦楚有誰知？

13.

October 5, 1911,
Required to Change Rooms, I Write These Words

Having just arrived at the wood house,
To get up and move again is really onerous.
I grab my baggage and hustle about,
Who could know this miserable first indignity?

14.

鬚眉七尺愧無伸，
蜷伏圈中俯仰人。
百般忍辱徒呼負，
斯人瀝空蒼天何？

14.

I, a seven-foot gentleman, am ashamed I cannot stretch out.
Corralled and concealed, curled in the center (like a worm),
    I bow and scrape to others.
One hundred ways to suffer humiliation, I cry defeat in vain.
This man's tears emptied, but what can
    the dark blue heavens do?

15.

來到木屋十日餘；
眼見有人撥回去。
令人見景亦生悲；
耗費金錢五千餘。
孤身飄流到此處；
不幸撥回父母悲；
咽吶的利息重重疊；
未知何日還清主。

15.

I've been at the wood house more than ten days.
My eyes witness people deported, preparing
        to return to China.
Look at their situation, these sad lives,
Squandering in excess of five thousand gold coins.

An orphan body drifted to this place.
Unlucky if I'm deported, my parents would be sad.
Interest fees would double and redouble.
I don't know when we could repay the lender.

16.

夙慕花旗幾優哉，
即時籌款動程來。
風波閱月已歷盡，
監牢居所受災磨。
仰望屋崙相咫尺，
願回祖國負耕鋤，
滿腹牢騷難寢寐，
聊書數句表心裁。

16.

I've long admired the Flower Flag as ultimately superior!
Immediately, I began raising money for my journey.
Already I've gone through a month of wind and waves,
Living in this prison is a disastrous ordeal.

Lifting my head, Oakland so close,
Yet I hope to return home to plow and hoe the fields.
Riddled with worry, it's hard to sleep well,
I depend upon books for lines of verse
        to express my broken heart.

17.

棄書荒硯來飄洋；
意欲把我素心揚。
難料到此遭囹圄；
壯志待酬抱恨長。
堪嘆來此如萍寄；
犧牲巨款受鬼劏。
此行深願酬我志；
否則囚困苦斷腸。

17.

Abandoning books and inkstone, I drifted across the sea,
My intention: to lift my humble self up to praise.
It was difficult to anticipate upon arrival,
    I'd encounter a locked jail,
My high hopes are compensated with endless rage.

Coming here, I must endure sighs as if mired in duckweed,
Having sacrificed a life's savings to the foreign devils.
For this journey, my deepest desire is
    for ambition to be rewarded,
But if not, a besieged inmate, bitter and heartbroken.

18.

浪跡江湖憶舊遊；
故人生死各千秋。
今生不幸為華裔；
忍辱含仇做楚囚。

18.

Having wandered homeless about the entire country,
    I remember former travels.
Old friends, living or dead,
    each with their own special qualities.
I am born unlucky, of Chinese descent,
So I must endure humiliation and contain hatred,
    just like a prisoner of Chu.

19.

居樓偶感

日處埃崙不自由；
蕭然身世混監囚。
牢騷滿腹憑詩寫；
塊壘撐胸借酒浮。
理悟盈虛因國弱；
道參消長為富求。
閒來別有疏狂想；
得允西奴登美洲。

19.

Staying in the Wood House

My days at Angel Island are without freedom,
Desolate circumstances, I mingle with prisoners.
Unhappy, my belly full of complaints, I rely on writing poems.
Clods of wall clog my chest, borrowed wine floats them free.

I'm aware of the laws of profit and loss because my nation weak,
Before long, my path vanishes in the pursuit of wealth.
When calm returns, there comes this wild, careless thought:
I've been granted permission from the western barbarian
      to enter America!

20.

深夜偶感

夜靜微聞風嘯聲，
形影傷情見景詠。
雲霧潺潺暗天，
蟲聲唧唧月微明。
悲苦相連天相遣，
愁人獨坐倚窗邊。

台山余題

20.

Deep Night

In the still of night, small sounds are a howling wind.
Shadows, an ache of old wounds, so I recite verse:

Fog and mist drift, a gloomy sky,
Insects rub crick-crack beneath the moon's faint light.
My sad and bitter face matches these heavens.
A worried man sits alone, leans at the window's sill.

Toishan (formerly known as Yee)

21.

讀罷詩書四五擔；
老來方得一青衫；
佳人問我年多少；
五十年前二十三。

21.

I stopped reading poetry and history after
      four or five ancient tomes.
An old man comes wearing a single blue shirt.
The beautiful female officer asks
      how many years have I,
Fifty years ago, it was but twenty three.

22.

此間囚困月重圓；
審問何時尚未知。
家窮逼我來受苦；
難盡心中憤與悲。
若得一審能上埠；
稍滅蠻夷百般欺；
倘能遂我平生願；
雖受苦楚亦唔拘。

22.

Since I've been confined, the moon has again waxed full,
When my interrogation, I don't yet know.
Family poverty forced me to come and suffer this bitterness.
It's difficult to empty one's heart of anger and sorrow.

If I could but enter San Francisco after one exam,
It wouldn't erase the barbarians' one hundred lies.
But if able to satisfy my life's dreams,
Even a little suffering wouldn't really matter.

23.

木屋拘留幾十天，
所囚墨例致牽連。
可惜英雄無用武，
只聽音來策祖鞭。

從今遠別此樓中，
各位鄉君眾歡同。
菓道其聞皆西式，
設成玉砌變如籠。

23.

Detained in the wood house several weeks,
It's because of Mexico's exclusion law which implicates me.
It's a pity heroes don't use weapons.
I await word to snap Zu's whip.

From here on, I'll travel far from this two-story building.
Each and every villager will share a happiness.
Don't idolize everything that's Western-style.
Even if cut from jade, these walls are
        nothing but a cage.

24.

舉筆寫詩我卿知；
昨夜三更嘆別離。
情濃囑語今猶在；
未知何日得旋歸。

24.

I raise a brush to write a poem to my dear wife:
Last night at third watch, a sigh of separation.
The deep affection you've expressed stays with me inside.
But I don't know when I can return to you.

25.

蠻夷發令把房遷，
上下奔馳氣絕然。
恰似干戈人心亂，
聲勢猶如走烽煙。

25.

The barbarian issued orders to change rooms.
Up and down, rushing about, I ran out of breath.
Just like in preparing for war, every mind a confusion.
A scene similar to the whirlwind stirred in beacon fire smoke.

26.

為口奔馳馳到監，
困愁愁食亦心煩。
薄待華人黃菜餐，
弱質難當實為難。

26.

Because of the mouth, frantically I rushed and landed in this jail.
Imprisoned, I worry. Even while eating, my heart is troubled.
Slim pickings for the Chinese, yellowed greens for a meal.
Such poor quality hard to accept, it's really hard!

27.

困囚木屋常愁悶；
憶別家鄉月幾圓。
家人倚望音書切；
憑誰傳語報平安？
木屋監囚愁悶多；
記憶來時歷苦楚；
過關未卜是何日；
空令歲月易蹉跎。

台山氏翁題

27.

Trapped in the wood house, I'm often sad and troubled,
I remember leaving the old village, several moons ago.
The relatives lean at the door, search for news from a letter.
Who can I rely upon to send a message that all is well?

In the wood house prisoners are mostly anxious and gloomy.
I remember when coming here a period of bitterness.
I can't predict the day I'll land,
Without a purpose, months and years easily
        become wasted time.

Old Man of Toishan

28.

囚困木屋天復天，
自由束縛豈堪言？
舉目誰歡惟靜坐，
關心自悶不成眠。
日永樽空愁莫解。
夜長枕冷清誰憐？
參透箇中孤苦味，
何如歸去學耕田？

28.

Locked in the wood house day after day,
My freedom restricted, how am I even capable of words?
I look for who's happy, but all sit quiet.
I'm tense and stressed, unable to sleep.

The days endless, my wineglass empty, but worry won't loosen.
The nights even longer, pillow cold; who'll take pity on me?
Fully knowing deep within this bitter loneliness,
Why not just go home and learn to plow the fields?

29.

中秋偶感

夜涼僵臥鐵床中，
窗前月姊透照儂。
悶來起立寒窗下，
愁把時計已秋中。
吾儕也應同敬賞，
菲儀無備亦羞容。

29.

Mid-Autumn Festival

Cool nights lying on the steel bunk.
Through a window, the moon goddess shines down on me.
Bored, I rise and stand beneath cold glass.
Anxious to stay on schedule, already mid-autumn.
I too should venerate her beauty.
Fragrant rites I've not readied, I'm so full of shame.

30.

西風吹動薄羅裳，
山坐高樓板木房。
意好子娘雲欲遠，
月明偏受夜更長。
床頭有酒心常醉，
枕底無花夢不香。
一幅幽情何心寄，
全憑知己解凄涼。

30.

The west wind drifts through my thin gauze shirt.
Against the hills, a tall building with plank-walled rooms.
I, wishing for my wife and son like clouds far away,
My night is even longer under the bright moon.

With wine at the head of the bed, my spirit always drunk,
Under a pillow, no flowered dreams or sweet.
One piece of quiet lives only in the heart.
I lean on others to lessen my bitter cool.

31.

陋室铭

山不在高，有仙则名。水不在深，有龙则灵。斯是陋室，惟吾德馨。苔痕上阶绿，草色入帘青。谈笑有鸿儒，往来无白丁。可以调素琴，阅金经。无丝竹之乱耳，无案牍之劳形。南阳诸葛庐，西蜀子云亭。孔子云：何陋之有？

刘禹锡

31.

Lou Shi Ming (Inscription About a Crude Dwelling)

Mountains do not need to be high; with immortals
    they are famed.
Streams do not need to be deep; with dragons
    they have spirit.
This is my crude room, but I am filled with fragrant virtue.

Moss marks the top of the stairs green;
    the color of grass enters the curtain's drab.
Speech and laughter like Confucian scholars;
    none with false pretensions.
You can play a silk zither, or read the golden classics.

No strings or bamboo flute to confuse the ear,
    no official records to mull over.
Like Zhuge Liang's hut in Nanyang,
Yang Xiong's Offspring of Clouds Pavilion in Western Shu.

Confucius once said, "When a gentleman lives there,
    what crudeness can it have?"

Liu Yuxi

32.

木屋銘

樓不在高，則明；
窗不在明，則遠；
島不在遠，則在。
煙治埃在，
嗟此木屋，
阻我行程。

四壁油漆綠，
週圍草色青。
喧嘩多鄉里，
守夜有巡丁。
可以施運動，
孔兄運動丁。

有孩子之勞耳，
無咕嚕之亂形。

南望醫生房，
西瞭陸軍營房。

作者云，「何樂之有？」

32.

Muhk Nguk Ming (Inscribed Upon the Wood House)

A building need not be tall; with windows, it will have light.
An island need not be far; here, Angel Island.
Alas, a wood building blocks my journey.

Four walls brushed green, contained by grass tinted green.
Inside, a cacophony of village dialects; night silenced
     by pale guards.
To make "luck" happen, the square-holed elder brother.

There are children to disturb the ears, but no speech
     to muddle over.
Towards the south, I observe the immigration hospital.
The west, an army camp.

This author says, "When a prisoner lives there,
     what happiness can it have?

33.

四壁蟲唧唧，
居人多歎息。
思及家中事，
不覺淚沾滴。

33.

Outside four walls, insects chirp,
From the residents inside, many sighs.
When thoughts turn to important family matters,
Without will, tears trickle then soak.

34.

少年子弟未知愁，
來到金山困木樓。
不悟眼前悲苦境，
還要終日戲如牛。

34.

Young children don't yet know worry.
Arriving in Gold Mountain to be confined at the wood house,
No awareness of the sad and bitter right before their eyes.
What's more, all day they must frolic like cattle.

35.

上年六月始揚帆；
不料今時到此監；
耗費金錢千數百。
生平孤苦累家兄。

35.

In June last year, I first set sail,
Not expecting that now I would be imprisoned.
I've squandered gold coins in the thousands and hundreds.
Born ordinary, alone and bitter,
    I've implicated elder brother.

36.

家徒壁立[][]留；
握別妻身[][]舟。
破浪乘風登墨[]；
[][][][][][]流。
不料浮萍至墨京；
寰球遍地已三年，
青蚨不識無傷我。
悶聽鎗林砲雨聲；
故冒偷關來居美；
誰知今日受囚刑？

36.

Nothing but bare walls at home [   ] stay,
I embraced my wife before leaving [   ] a boat.
Through breaking waves, we rode favorable winds
        to Mexico [   ],
[   ] roam.
I never thought I'd drift like duckweed to Mexico City,
I've wandered the world for three years.
That I knew not copper coin did not hurt me.
But I grew depressed listening to fusillade of rifle fire
        and cannon shot,
Reason enough to sneak a mountain pass, to live in America,
But who knew today I'd secure a prisoner's fate?

37.

李宅人員把身抽；

季夏乘船到美洲。

海過舟灣候上岸；

紀錄無辜困木樓。

念及事情心厭悶；

詩章題首解愁憂。

目下未曾批消案；

錄記情由實可嘲。

在坐虛延長歲月；

此處如籠一隻鳩。

華僑[]鐵城山僧題贈

37.

I, a member of the Lee household, prepared to leave,
By summer's end, had traveled by ship to America.
Having crossed, the ship docked, I waited to go ashore,
Innocent but lacking documents, I'm trapped
        in the wood building.
Thinking of these emotional ordeals, my spirit sinks,
I compose poetry to unknot worry and grief.
I note that my petition hasn't yet been denied,
But writing down these words makes real my anger.
Sitting here in vain, delayed long years and months,
This place is like a cage where one pigeon lives.

Mountain Monk, an overseas Chinese
from the City of Iron

38.

風清月朗可憐宵;
木屋孤衾倍寂寥。
客有鄉思眼伴柳;
卿無旅意窗戀蕉。
素娥未曉人間苦;
白種偏囚東椏僑。
不若村民耕與讀;
優悠柴米樂簞瓢。

38.

Clear breezes, a brilliant moon, make for a pitiful night,
In the wood house, a single quilt shrouds an emptiness.
A homesick traveler thinks of his companion willow,
A wife, with no desire to leave, loved the banana palm
    outside the window.

Su'e never dawned in the space of human suffering.
Whites make prisoners out of Dongya visitors,
Unlike villagers who plow and study,
Excellent long firewood, and the rice happy
    in basket and gourd.

39.

今日為冬末，
明朝是春分。
交替兩年景，
愁煞木樓人。

39.

Today, the end of winter,
Tomorrow morning, the spring divide.
One year's circumstance is replaced by another's
Worries to death the man in a wooden barrack.

40.

水景如苔千里曲，
陸路無涯路步難。
平風到埠心如是，
安樂誰知住木樓。

40.

A waterscape like kelp entwined a thousand li,
The shore path with no bank is difficult to walk.
Calm breezes enter the heart of the city, as they should.
Such tranquility and joy, who knows I reside
　　　in a wooden barrack?

III. HOOKWORMS

41.

詳恨番奴不奉公，
頻施苛例逞英雄。
凌虐華僑兼背約，
百般專制驗勾蟲。

41.

I totally despise the foreign barbarians who have
      no respect for fairness.
Often they make harsh rules to strut their manliness.
They cruelly mistreat we overseas Chinese, and break treaties.
One hundred kinds of autocratic acts and then
      to check for hookworms.

42.

想起愁來題首詩。

因為家窮走花旗。

只望到來登岸易；

誰知番人轉例規？

刺耳驗血兼驗屎；

影有勾蟲要調治。

取得洋蚨數十餘；

困在醫房苦愁悲。

未知何日得痊癒。

若得脫身要念志，

一排走清唔向倚，

免至凌辱受鬼欺；

梓里一看宜謹記；

寫我狂言留後知。

42.

Random thoughts, my worry returned which became this poem.
Because my family poor, I left for the Land of the Flower Flag.
I'd only thought in coming here, I'd land easily,
Who knew the barbarians would change
        their rules and regulations?
Ear pricks, blood tests, and exams of feces,
A trace of hookworm triggers the transfer protocol.
They took more than ten foreign dollars,
Trapped in this hospital ward, I'm bitter and sad.
I don't know when I'll be healed,
Hoping for discharge, my body is determined.
One wing found clear of disease, no longer requiring treatment.
You must avoid insults from the bullying ghosts.
Fellow villagers, be watchful and remember to take care:
I write my insane speech to let those
        who'll come after know.

43.

忝屬同群事感哀。
訃音誰遞故鄉回?
痛君騎鶴歸冥去;
有客乘槎赴美來。
淚鎖孤魂悲杜宇;
愁牽旅夢到陽台。
可憐藥石施醫誤;
險被焚屍一炬灰。

43.

This humblest of our group feels sorrow.
Who will report the news of your death back to the old village?
The supreme pain of you riding the crane back to
    the dark realms;
Once, a sojourner rode on a raft to come visit America.

Tears chain the lonely soul, the cuckoo's mournful cry;
Worry has led to dreams of arriving at the Terrace of Yang.
It's pitiful that the medicine was given mistakenly;
For safety, your corpse burned to ash.

44.

噩耗傳聞實可哀，
弔君何日裹屍回？
無能瞑目憑誰訴？
有識應知悔此來，
千古含愁千古恨，
思鄉空對望鄉臺。
未酬壯志埋壞土，
知爾雄心死不灰。

44.

Shocking news, I was truly sad,
To respectfully mourn, when will they wrap
      your corpse for return?
Unable to close your eyes, who will you lean on to see?
You should've known you'd regret coming here.

A thousand old worries recalled, a thousand old resentments,
Thinking of the village is to look emptily towards
      the Terrace for Gazing Homeward.
Your high hopes unrewarded, buried in wrong earth,
Yet know, great ambition may die but will never turn to ash.

45.

半生逐逐為求名，
借問何時可愜情？
藥石無靈成瘰疾，
岐黃未遇卻心驚。
蒼天想必神能佑，
丹鼎無需病自平。
從此聞飆雲漢起，
行看萬里奮鵬程。

45.

Half a life spent running back and forth searching for fame,
I ask myself when will I be satisfied?
Medicines were of no effect as I fought through malaria.
I never met the Huang deity, but my heart was fearful.

In the gray heavens, surely the gods watched over me.
No need for an alchemist's crucible, the illness resolved itself.
From now on, when I hear whirlwinds stir in the Milky Way,
I'll travel ten thousand li, strive for the journey of the *peng*.

IV. PEARL-LIKE TEARS WILL FALL

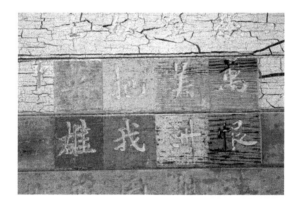

46.

揖別知己出外洋；
豈知胡虜困我身？
自古強權無公禮；
有何妙策出牢籠。
一旦撥回歸去國；
數月工程付水中。
可惜馮唐容易老；
何其李廣最難封？

46.

I said farewell to my closest friends upon leaving for overseas.
How was I to know the barbarians would confine me?
Since ancient times, there's been absolute power without justice.
What clever plan do I have to escape this prison cage?

One morning if I'm deported and must return,
Consider months of effort tossed into the seas.
It's a pity Feng Tang's face grew old.
Why so difficult for Li Guang to be conferred a title?

47.

埃崙居處日添愁；
面亦黃兮身亦瘦。
留難批消磨猶未了；
最怕陳題打回頭。

47.

Each day at Angel Island adds to my worry,
My face sallow, the body gaunt.
To stay, the deliberations linger as if yet unfinished.
My greatest fear: my petition eliminated, and I turned back.

Chan

48.

斗門人往大溪地，
來到木屋十餘日。
溪地有人回唐山，
誰知此埠極難為。
有人回來有人去，
使枉洋銀三百餘。
不到此埠心不忿，
回家父母苦極悲。
留下利息重重疊，
未知何日還他主？

48.

Doumen people depart for Tahiti,
Having come to the wood house over ten days ago.
Yet Tahiti has men returning to Tang Mountain,
Who knew this port so difficult to enter?
Some men arrive, others leave,
I've wasted over three hundred foreign silver dollars.
To never see the heart of this city, I've no anger,
But to return home to my parents, all bitterness and grief.
To stay, the interest piles up,
Don't know when I can ever repay the lender.

49.

批消半載無消息；
誰知今日撥回唐？
船中捱浪珠淚落；
清夜三思苦難堪。

49.

My petition denied already half a year with no further news.
Who knew that today, I would be deported back
      to Tang Mountain?
At mid-ship, I'll suffer waves, and pearl-like tears will fall.
On a clear night, three times I'll find the bitterness hard to bear.

50.

埃崙半載同甘苦；
我今撥回始別離，
寄語同鄉上埠日；
務望時記是中朝。

50.

For half a year on Angel Island, we knew both bitter and sweet;
Now I am ordered deported and packing to leave,
Send word to fellow villagers that when they land;
Look forward to the day, when they'll remember
        we were here.

Poem 59

51.

林到美洲，
逮入木樓。
成為囚犯，
來此一秋。
美人不准，
批撥回頭。
消息報告，
回國驚憂。
國弱華人，
嘆不自由。
鐵城道人題。

51.

I, Lum, arrived in America, entered the wooden barracks.
Having served as prisoner for a crime already one autumn.
The Americans barred me, ordered me deported.
When the news was given, to return to my country is worrisome.
Our nation weak, we Chinese sigh at the lack of freedom.

Iron City Taoist

52.

新客到美洲；
必逮入木樓。
儼如大犯樣；
在此經一秋。
美國人不准；
批消撥回頭。
船中波浪大；
回國實堪憂。
國弱我華人；
苦嘆不自由。
我國豪強日；
誓斬胡人頭。

52.

When a new guest arrives in America, surely
    he'll be confined in the wooden barrack.
Grave as if he'd committed a great crime,
    myself here already one autumn.

The Americans barred me,
    ordered me deported and sent back.
At midship, huge waves,
    to return to my country is truly filled with grief.

The nation weak, we Chinese sigh bitterly at
    the lack of freedom.
The day my country becomes strong, I swear to
    cut off the barbarians' heads.

53.

埃崙偶感

飄零湖海倏經秋；
萬劫縈過作楚囚。
伍子吹簫懷雪恨；
蘇卿持節誓報仇。
霽雲射矢非多事；
勾踐臥薪卻有由。
激烈肝腸輕一決；
蒼天諾否此志酬。
台山助苗長者題

53.

Occasional Feelings on Angel Island

Floating alone at sea, autumn flew by,
Ten thousand calamities I've just gone through,
    like a prisoner from Chu.
When Wu Zi blew on his panpipes,
    he wished to air away regret,
As Master Su Qing gripped his tasseled staff,
    he took an oath of revenge.
When Jiyun launched his arrow,
    it was not an extraneous matter,
Goujian slept on firewood, but with good reason.
My incited liver and guts fire a singular determination,
Will the dark blue heavens assent to
    this desire to repay?

Toishan Senior Advising the Young

54.

尚存一息志無灰，
敬勖同堂眾楚材。
知恥便能將恥雪，
揮戈方可免戈裁。
莫道無謀芟醜虜，
思求有術把天回。
男兒十萬橫磨劍，
誓斬樓蘭闢草萊。

54.

If you've one breath left, don't let your hopes turn to ash,
I respectfully exhort my barrackmates, cut from
      the timber of Chu.
To directly face disgrace is to wipe away shame,
Brandishing a spear at one's side avoids being pierced.

Don't say there's no means to mow down the ugly barbarians,
Think of a way to turn heaven around.
All about, a hundred thousand brothers and sons
      sharpen their swords,
Swearing to behead the Loulan,
      and slash away the grassy weeds.

55.

美有強權無公理，
圖圉吾人也罹辜。
不由分說真殘酷，
俯首回思莫奈何。
陳題

55.

Americans have unbridled power but lack guiding principles.
They confine us as if we were criminals.
Without any explanation, it's truly oppressive.
I bow my head in reflection, but it will have no effect.

Chan

56.

輕武重文嗟古風，
挽正鋤奸惜來遲。
羈此儆知因國弱，
眠錐應勵振邦雄。

56.

Demeaning the military and praising the literary are old habits,
It's a pity I've come too late to get rid of the traitors.
Confined here, I know it's because the country is weak.
Sleeping with awls: a way to arouse a nation's heroes.

57.

埃屋三椽聊保身，

崙麓積愫不堪陳。

待得飛騰順遂日，

剷除關稅不論仁。

台山人題

57.

Angel's wood house of three rafters merely shelters the body.
Island foothills contain stories impossible to share.
Wait to spin somersaults on my approval day,
Raze the immigration station without speaking of benevolence!

Toishan Man

58.

同病相憐如一身，
恰似仲尼困在陳。
私維君心仗義力，
足戮胡奴弗讓仁。
辛和

58.

I sympathize, the same illness, as if we shared a body,
Just like Confucius surrounded at the State of Chen.
Privately, I believe a nation should rely upon
        righteousness for power,
But to trample the barbarians would not be inhumane.

                                    Sun in response

蛟龍失水螻蟻欺，
猛虎遭囚小兒戲。
被困安敢與爭雄，
得勢復仇定有期。

Carved in reverse upon the wall...

蛟龍失水螻蟻欺，
猛虎遭囚小兒戲。
被困安敢與爭雄，
得勢復仇定有期。

59.

Out of the water, the legendary sea dragon is bullied by ants,
The fierce tiger, unluckily caged, mocked by children.
Trapped and docile, do I dare strive to be the hero?
When I have power, my moment of revenge
      will surely arrive!

60.

握別兄弟與同窗；
為口奔馳涉美洋。
豈知西奴心理喪；
百般苛例虐我唐。
數次審查猶未了，
還須裸體驗胸膛。
我們同胞遭至此，
皆因國勢未能張，
倘得中華一統日。
定割西奴心與腸。

60.

I clasped hands in parting with my brothers and classmates.
Because of the mouth waded swiftly across the Pacific.
Who knew the Western barbarians bereft
      of compassion or reason?
One hundred cases of petty abuse against the Tang.
Countless interrogations, and still not done.
What's more, must stand naked, just to check the lungs.
Compatriots, we've come to this,
All because our nation's power too weak to protect.
Come that day when China unites,
I myself will rip out the barbarian's heart and guts.

61.

假道呂宋走花旗，
關情嚴密不知機。
監牢木屋囚困日，
波斯鐵船被撥期。
窮途阮籍誰憐哭？
絕域李陵空嘆愁，
無可奈何事制厄，
命蹇時乖受此磨。

61.

An evasive path to Mexico through the United States,
But the border was closed tight, and
      I was unaware of the situation.
Locked up in the wood house a prisoner for days.
I'm assigned to the steel ship *Persia* for deportation.

When Ruan Ji walked in poverty, who would take pity or cry?
In a remote land far away, Li Ling emptied a worried sigh.
Helpless and unable, of what use is it to pretend?
Crippled by fate, my time better spent
      accepting this reversal.

62.

感景拙詠

滄海圍孤峰，
崎嶇困牢籠。
鳥疏寒山緻，
鴻使莫尋蹤。
留難經半載，
愁恨積滿容，
今將歸國去，
空勞精衛功。

62.

Perceiving the Landscape, I Compose This Worthless Verse

Blue-green ocean encircles a solitary peak,
Rugged hills edge this prison cage.
Birds to avoid cold mountain fineries,
Wild geese make no trace.

Landing has been hard for more than half a year,
My face flushed with hatred and worry.
Now I must return to my country
Like the jingwei bird having toiled in empty air.

VI. CONSOLATION AND EXHORTATION

Poems 19, 67 and 10
Men's Barracks, Room 205

63.

香山許生自慰題

壁上題詩過百篇，
看來皆是嘆迍邅。
愁人曷向愁人訴，
蹇客偏思蹇客憐。
得失豈知原有命，
富貧誰謂不由天。
此間困處何須怨，
自由英雄每厄先。

63.

Self-Consolation

On these walls, over a hundred poems.
They all seem to lament a lack of progress.
What can a single worried man say to another?
Unfortunate travelers lean on same others for sympathy.

Win or lose, how can one know in advance one's fate?
Rich or poor, who's to say it's not the will of heaven?
Of this confinement, should I complain?
Every self-made hero must first face adversity.

Heungshan-born Hui

64.

勸君切勿來偷關，
四圍綠水繞青山。
登高遠望無涯岸，
欲渡綠水難上難。

生命堪虞君自重，
斯言不是作為閒。
盡任撥回歸國去？
覓些營生揾兩餐。

64.

I wouldn't advise you under any circumstances
     to steal across the fence.
On every side, blue-green seas surround new green hills.
Rise high and peer into the distance, no cliffs.
Aching to ferry across green creates hardship upon hardship.

Life is worrisome, and you should be poised.
This advice is not given casually.
Why not let them deport you back to China?
Find some work to make a living and get by on two meals.

65.

兩經滄海歷風塵，
木屋羈留倍痛深。
國弱巫當齊努力，
狂瀾待挽仗同群。

65.

Twice I've crossed the blue-green ocean,
    navigating wind and dust.
This wood house contains double pain and deep sorrow.
For a weak country, it's appropriate to band together
    to seek power.
To turn back the wild wave, we must draw weapons as one.

66.

特勸同胞不可憂，
雖然被困在木樓。
他日中華興轉後，
擅用炸彈滅美洲。

66.

Special advice to my compatriots: don't worry,
Although it's true we're trapped here in the wooden barrack.
The day that China begins to turn it around,
Expertly she'll use bombs to obliterate America.

67.

寄語同居勿過憂，
且把閒愁付水流。
小受折磨非是苦，
破崙曾被島中囚。

67.

I send word to my barrack mates, do not be sad,
What's more, gather your idle worries and entrust them
      to the flowing stream.
Don't let a little hardship make you bitter,
Once even Napoleon, held upon an island a prisoner.

68.

壁牆題詠萬千千，
盡皆此牢怨語及愁言。
若卸此牢升騰日，
要憶當年有個編。
日用所需宜省儉，
無為奢侈誤青年。
幸我同胞牢緊念，
得些微利早回旋。

香山題

68.

On these walls are etched tens of thousands of poems,
In every case, they are cries of complaint and worried words.
Assuming my release from prison on approval day,
It's essential to recall the tenor of this year.

For daily necessities, save and be frugal,
Avoid the wasteful extravagances of youth.
My fellow detainees be mindful:
Take a few small gains, then make an early return.

Heungshan

69.

雄鷹亦易馴，
能屈始能伸。
也歷千年劫，
曾困七日陳。
偉人多本色，
名士樂天真。
得失縈懷抱，
心猿證悟禪。

69.

[   ] male eagle also easy to tame,
[   ] be able to bend before one is able to stretch.
[   ] experience a thousand years of calamities,
[   ] once surrounded for seven days we're told.

[   ] great men are often a natural color,
[   ] named scholars happy to be themselves.
[   ] gain and loss entangled inside my breast,
[   ] monkey mind belies an awareness of simplicity.

70.

香山許生勉客題

說去花旗喜溢顏，
千金羅掘不辭艱。
親離有話喉先哽，
妻別多情淚對潸。
浪大如山頻駭客，
政苛似虎倍嘗蠻。
毋忘此日君登岸，
發奮前程莫懶閒。

70.

Shew of Heungshan Exhorts the Sojourner

When talking of going to the Land of the Flower Flag,
      my face beamed with happiness,
I dug up 1,000 gold pieces but leaving more difficult.
Saying goodbye to my parents, I choked with sadness,
When parting from my wife, many feelings and shared tears.

Frequently, waves big as mountains terrified us travelers,
Petty bureaucracy, like a tiger, doubles the barbarians' bite.
Never forget this day when you go ashore,
Push hard on your journey, don't be lazy or idle.

The Wood House
Men's Barracks, Angel Island Immigration Station

NOTES

1.5 "white jade": known in China as "mutton fat" jade, a variety of nephrite found in a creamy white coloring. Nephrite also exists in a variety of green tones, but the gemstone jadeite is even rarer and its translucent emerald-green hue most valued.

1.7 "li": a Chinese measurement of distance, approximately one third of a mile. The measure of 10,000 li is close to the geographical distance between Hong Kong and San Francisco.

1.10 "weighty green coin": metal in Chinese coins made of bronze or brass, when oxidized would develop a greenish patina.

2.2 "jabbing an awl into my thigh": a reference to the life of Su Qin, a scholar during the Warring States period. This phrase is derived from a Chinese idiom 懸梁刺股 that can be transliterated into Cantonese as "yyuhn leuhng chi gu" and translated word-for-word into English as "hang beam thorn thigh." The phrase invokes the story of when Su Qin tried to prevent himself from falling asleep while studying for long hours by stabbing himself in the thigh with a sharp instrument, epitomizing extreme diligence and concentrated effort.

3.3 "Land of the Flower Flag": 花旗 or "Fa Keih" ("Flower Flag") describes the American flag with its stars and stripes symbols, giving this phrase its meaning as a colloquialism for the United States.

4.1 "Hèung Sèhng": this district administrative center of old Heungshan County was also known as 鐵城 or "Tit Sèhng," the City of Iron. It is now part of the prefecture-level city of Zhongshan in southern Guangdong Province.

4.4 "Gold Mountain": 金山 or "Gām Sàan" was a popular Chinese name for California. It derived from the early participation of thousands of Chinese miners in the state's Gold Rush of 1849. Anti-Chinese discrimination first began in those goldfields with the passage of the

Foreign Miner's Tax, meant to discourage international competition to white American miners.

4.9 The year cited is 1924. Year dating in ancient China was based upon dynastic eras; each founding year was designated a "Year One." While the Chinese Revolution of 1911 was not feudal in nature, this tradition partly continued during the early 20th century until the modern use of the Gregorian calendar took full effect.

5 This is one of the few poems whose author is not anonymous. It is attributed to Smiley Jann, an Angel Island detainee who had copied many of the wall inscriptions into a notebook for preservation's sake. Jann's collection is one of two written sources for the wall poetry and comprises much of what's available, other than that yet discoverable on the actual walls. Many poems are missing in whole or part from the men's barracks. Angel Island officials used paint and putty to intentionally erase detainee poetry underscoring the importance of Jann and Tet Yee's curatorial efforts.

Jann's own poem is not one found on the walls; when he wrote his poem is also unknown. Some Angel Island poems were in fact first published in print: in China, San Francisco Chinatown or elsewhere. One such poem is the long narrative "Detention in the Muk Uk," first published in a Chinese newspaper less than two months after the Angel Island Immigration Station's opening. This poem was translated by Marlon K. Hom and is included alongside its original in the essential resource, *Island: Poetry and History of Chinese Immigrants on Angel Island 1910-1940*, 2nd edition. Other Angel Island-related poetry, including work in the "folk song" tradition, appear in Hom's own book *Songs from Gold Mountain: Cantonese Rhymes from San Francisco Chinatown*.

6.3 "meeting the elders": General Xiang Yu (232-202 BCE) at the end of the Qin dynasty in the 3rd century BCE, led 8,000 young soldiers to conquer China. The legend is that after nearly losing all his men to Liu Bang, the eventual founder of the Han dynasty, Xiang Yu chose suicide rather than return home in defeat to face the elders.

7.4 "Seventh Day of the Seventh Moon": a reference to the Qiqiao Festival celebrated among Chinese. It commemorates the annual meeting of the cowherd and weaver girl in Chinese mythology and encompasses the theme of separation from loved ones. Here it is used to reference leaving the ancestral home. See Names and Terms, "Qiqiao Festival."

7.9 "wood house": 木樓 or "muhk lauh" is a wooden building with at least two stories. The term refers to the Immigration Station men's barracks, site of most of the Angel Island wall poems. Another popular term used in the wall poetry for the men's barracks is 木屋 or "muhk uhk" which literally means "wood house."

7.10 "barbarians": the term 番奴 or "foreign slaves" originally referred to the non-Han Chinese invaders who at various times ruled China. It is used here derogatorily for Westerners and reflects the resentment felt by the Chinese for the European, Japanese and American-established "spheres of influence" where foreign powers carved up China for imperialist exploitation.

8.5 "sigh like lonely orphans": the phrase 歎孤單 or "sigh orphan individual" appears not infrequently in these poems and evokes a detainee feeling of isolation from home and family. Chinese society is family-based and communal, so the long sojourn to America and the enforced separation of husbands and wives at Angel Island were all circumstances that felt intolerable especially for persons with lengthy stays.

8.7 "Tang Mountain": the term 唐山 or "Tohng Saan" is another Cantonese colloquialism for China. The Cantonese consider themselves descendants of the Tang people who ruled during the Tang dynasty. Although the soundscape of the Tang dialect is no longer known, some theorize that it's likely closer to modern Cantonese as opposed to the Beijing-based national standard of Mandarin. Other linguists say that many of the hundred plus Chinese dialects are in fact separate languages based upon a criterion of mutual unintelligibility. At Angel Island,

Toishan immigrants could barely understand barrackmates who spoke the Heungshan tongue, and vice versa, creating a "House of Babel" effect.

10.4 "wild geese sorrow": the poem opens with classical Tang poetic descriptions of nature to thematically explore relationships between self and world. Of particular note is the phrase 雁哀 or "ngaan oi" which I've translated as "wild geese sorrow," evoking the loneliness of geese migrating great distances both leaving from and returning home. The detainees might easily have witnessed migratory waterfowl stopping upon San Francisco Bay while traveling the Pacific Flyway.

11.1 "island of immortals": this Chinese name for Angel Island makes reference to a cultural near-equivalent of "immortals" for angels. In Chinese cosmology, no divine beings act as messengers for a supreme power, but there are immortals considered divine. The popular Taoist legend of the Eight Immortals situates their place of residence on Penglai Mountain-Island.

12.3 "Island": the term 埃崙 or "Aai Leuhn" is a transliteration of the name "Angel Island" and was a colloquial designation used by the Cantonese immigrants.

13 Detainees were occasionally reassigned to new rooms with very little notice, a source of irritation as they had to pack their bags and belongings quickly and move. This minor annoyance underscored their status as prisoners, lacking control of living space and in a larger sense, of their own lives.

14.1-3 This poet comments upon the cramped quarters in the men's barracks, laid out dormitory-style with rows of three-tiered bunk beds in close proximity. Anywhere from 200-300 persons could be housed in the barracks at any given time, far more than the rooms were designed to accommodate.

15 Individuals and families spent great sums to send someone to the United States, often selling off property or borrowing from relatives and

moneylenders to obtain the necessary cash. Loans had to be repaid and with interest whether the journey was successful or not, though some relief was given for deportees. Funds were used to pay for housing, ship passage, coaching documents, and the right to use a particular identity. Varying cash amounts were cited in different wall poems, but needless to say, the financial burden was onerous for these mostly impoverished immigrants.

15.1 "wood house": 木屋, or "muhk uhk" was a popular term for the Immigration Station's men's barracks. With its Douglas Fir construction, it is the main site for the wall inscriptions. Prior to the opening of the Angel Island facility in 1910, Chinese immigrants were processed at another "wood house" located upon a pier at the Embarcadero in San Francisco. This poem uses the Cantonese pronunciation for assonant rhyming (mù wū in Pinyin also works in the assonant rhyme scheme).

16.5 "Oakland": from his vantage point in China Cove with its northeast view, this speaker is probably observing what today are the cities of Pt. Richmond and Richmond and not Oakland which is in the East Bay. However Oakland Chinatown was well known to Chinese immigrants and this image visualizes a tantalizingly close mainland horizon, which on a clear San Francisco Bay Area day may seem just yards away.

17.6 "mired in duckweed": an image that appears in several poems and most likely derives from the alluvial plains of the Pearl River Delta with its sloughs and backwaters. To be so mired is to be clogged, unable to move, stuck, like a small boat which cannot go forward or backwards because of excess vegetation.

17.7 "foreign devils": the terms 番鬼 or "faan gwai" ("foreign devils") and 鬼佬 or "gwai lou" ("devil person") were vernacular Cantonese terms for white people, who ironically were seen as "foreigners" even though it was the Chinese who were migrating to America to live and work. Of course, the first-generation immigrant's frame of reference was rooted in his homeland.

18.7 "prisoner of Chu": the term 做 楚 囚 or "zauh cho chauh" is to be a held prisoner, a person doing hard time.

20.7 "Toishan": here the poet has adopted the name of his ancestral district for a pseudonym. Cantonese immigrants had strong social and familial ties with their villages and farmlands and often relocated to enclaves in the United States where established communities spoke their own dialect.

21.1-2 Perhaps a reference to two of the Confucian classics: Shi Jing (Classic of Poetry) and Shu Jing (Classic of History), books which in ancient times were often large and bulky.

21.3 Chinese peasants and workers traditionally wore clothing colored blue or gray.

21.4 "beautiful female officer": the words 佳 人 or "gaai yahn" literally means "beautiful person," which is a pun on the term 美 人 or "mei yahn," which means an "American."

23.2 In 1921 the Mexican government issued its own ban on Chinese immigration. Angel Island also served as a detention facility for transit to and from Cuba, Mexico and other Latin American countries.

23.4 "Zu's whip": is a contraction of "the whip of Zu Di." Zu Ti 祖 逖 (266-321 CE) was a general during the Western Jin dynasty (256-316 CE). A footnote in Island states that General Zu Ti once swore to recover lost territory seized by non-Chinese invaders. Another general, also a friend, said, "I sleep with my weapon awaiting the dawn. My ambition is to kill the barbarian enemy, but I am always afraid that Zu will crack the whip before me." So this reference means to be focused and compete to be first.

23.7 "Western style": post-Revolution of 1911 and during the May 4th Movement, Chinese intellectuals rigorously debated the correct road for China's impending modernization, whether to follow Western culture and its capitalist economic systems or to create a separate Chinese path based upon native cultural traditions. As in developing nations today, conflicts between industrialization and tradition remain real and vexing.

24.2 "third watch": this is one of the few poems that directly address personal relationships, here between husband and wife. While at Angel Island, Chinese husbands and wives were housed in separate barracks, and any contact was discouraged to prevent collusion and outside coaching in the interrogation process. This image is based upon a practice in traditional Chinese villages, where a night watchman banged his gong at appointed hours (e.g. 3rd watch) to indicate that all was well. So this husband, unable to sleep, has turned to writing his feelings in poetry.

At times one spouse might be approved to land while the other, whose status was yet pending, was left behind; the infamous case of Soto Shee is an extreme example. After her husband left for San Francisco, Soto Shee stayed and her infant died at Angel Island. Grieving alone and in despair, she attempted suicide but fortunately was discovered and rescued. After her own landing, she went on to live a happy American life with many children and grandchildren.

25.4 "beacon fire smoke": in ancient China, watchtowers were erected at strategic points along the extended frontier. When invasions occurred, bonfires were lit upon these towers, and the ensuing smoke would warn the populace of a state of war.

26.3 "yellowed greens": a reference to wilted leaves of cheap cabbage that were initially served to the detainees, resulting in "food riots." Detainees claimed that Angel Island officials were underfunding their food budget and the cooks were scraping by with low quality food. Such a diet on a regular basis would seem monotonous and unpalatable.

27.3 Chinese immigrants would often send word home by mail or sometimes through friends and relatives on their status in America. Because this kind of communication was extremely slow, months might pass before hearing from a loved one.

29 "Mid-Autumn Festival": this annual event occurs on the 15th day of the 9th month in the lunar calendar and marks the celebration of the Fall harvest. The setting of this poem is reminiscent of the classical Tang poet Li Bai's poem "Moonlit Night," where a solitary speaker wakes from sleep, peers up at the moon and has a sudden revelation.

Much of the Angel Island poetry borrows tropes and forms from Heng-t'ang-t'ui-shih's *Tang shih san pai shou* (唐詩三百首) or *Three Hundred Tang Poems*, a compendium of some of the greatest Tang poems by writers such as Du Fu, Li Bai, Wang Wei, Li Shangyin and Meng Haoran. These poems were most likely taught to the Angel Island poets as part of their language arts education and continue to be part of the basic curriculum for Chinese students around the world today.

30   This lyric poem is resplendent with Tang-style nature imagery (clouds, moon) and Taoist philosophy (spirit, heart). Its last line underscores the solace fellow detainees often gave one another and perhaps derived from reading the poetry on the barrack walls.

31 "Lou Shi Ming": in this classical poem Liu Yuxi (772-842 CE) argues how the value of a Confucian scholar's "crude dwelling" cannot be measured by the rough nature of its material circumstance but instead by the right living of its owner. A typical Tang poem, these lines incorporate nature images (mountains, streams) and historical figures. The poem's strategy uses juxtaposition to elucidate its philosophical meaning. Though not an Angel Island wall poem, it is the inspiration for an imitation made by a detainee poet in Poem 32.

32 "Muhk Nguk Ming": in the age-old practice of artistic borrowing, this composition mimics the form of the preceding poem "Lou Shi Ming." Imitation is oft used by young artists to develop craft techniques but also to pay homage to exemplary work. Here the poet adheres closely to Poem 31's form but fills it with content from his own immigrant experience. He indirectly contrasts the harsh men's barracks environs to the humble but noble one described in the earlier Tang poem.

This poet's overall conclusion is opposite to that of Liu Yuxi's; surroundings do in fact make the person and not vice versa. Yet on a metaphorical level, one might say that this detainee's act of writing poetry, of turning his oppressive experience into art, has elevated suffering to a higher level of spirit and is therefore redemptive in nature.

32.7 "square-holed elder brother": a reference to traditional Chinese coins that had square holes at their center. Even at the men's barracks, money was a grease to could make things happen, e.g. detainees might bribe Chinese chefs who commuted daily from San Francisco Chinatown to bring them roast duck, newspapers, and cigarettes.

34 Young children and teens detained at Angel Island often accompanied their mothers to housing in the women's quarters at the Administration Building. In oral interviews, they shared that their experience was different than that of adults, often seeing the journey as an adventure of sorts, and they didn't seem to mind the food or boredom as much. This poet is a little peeved by their antics.

35.5 "I've implicated elder brother": this poem illustrates the collective nature of immigration, where family members combine resources to send one of their own overseas. Here the speaker carries guilt from the monetary debt owed to his older sibling.

36 So many of the Angel Island poems, like poems from classical antiquity, exist only in fragments. The Chinese original was carved in its traditional vertical layout, so that its first lines which are on the right, have characters that are unreadable or missing. Poems have been obscured by poor carving, deterioration, censorship, or even construction work on the building. Here, the randomness of missing characters suggests some type of physical wall damage. However, it can be inferred from the remaining text that the speaker's family was poor, and he had to leave for Mexico to earn a living. Gunfire references in lines 8-9 probably relate to the Mexican civil wars.

38.6 "Su'e": better known as Chang'e, the moon goddess. See Names and Terms, "Chang'e."

38.7 "Dongya": 東椏 is a village in the Heungshan district and perhaps the ancestral home of the poet. By removing the "tree" radical in the second character, one ends up with the phrase 東亞 or "East Asia." (My own maternal ancestral village is 西椏 or Sai Aa which is about a mile from Dongya.)

39.2 "spring divide": this occasional poem may have been composed at the Spring equinox (June) but for Chinese writers, more likely upon the Lunar New Year which occurs on the second new moon after the winter solstice (in January-February). The Lunar New Year culturally marks the end of winter and beginning of spring. Two years of waiting is a long time.

41.6 "hookworms": detainees were subject to medical examinations prior to receiving approval to land. One public health test was for hookworms. At first detainees found with infestation by the parasite were deported. Later patients could elect to receive medical treatment at the Angel Island Hospital upon payment of a fee.

42 This poem clearly delineates the medical exam process at Angel Island. Ear pricks and fecal exams were for filariasis and uncinariasis. The testing, any required treatments and waiting to be cleared of disease were very stressful for the detainees.

43 This particular poem and its companion, Poem 44, were most likely written about the death of the same individual, though apparently composed by different persons. A common exercise in Chinese poetry was for different writers to compose verse on the same subject, with the added challenge of using the same poetic forms or rhyming words, a kind of collaboration. This might be for entertainment accompanied with much wine and merriment, although here the subject is clearly somber.

43.3 "riding the crane": the symbol of the crane represents death. In Chinese mythology, cranes brought immortals to their palace-island residence. This poem is replete with Chinese historical allusions. There is documentation that a number of Angel Island detainees died while awaiting approval to land.

43.7 "Terrace of Yang": 陽台 or "yeuhng toih" ("male platform") is a common metaphor for a place for lovers' trysts. The phrase derives from Song Yu's "Rhapsody on the High Terrace" where King Huai of Chu (328-299 BCE) met the spirit of Shamanka Mountain in a dream and had sexual relations with her.

44.8 "Terrace for Gazing Homeward": a place where one could ascend to gaze in the direction of his or her former home. This phrase originated in a story from the Western Jin dynasty about two princesses who fled to a distant region and married commoners in a village. They were homesick so their fellow villagers built a terrace for them to gaze in the direction of their home.

45.6 "alchemist's crucible": the primary dream of ancient Chinese alchemists was to discover the pill of immortality. In one Taoist experiment, cinnabar and other chemicals were heated in a crucible which would produce the liquid, mercury; hence, the term 辰砂坩堝 or "cinnabar crucible."

45.8 "journey of the peng": the peng 鵬 is a giant bird that transforms from a giant fish in Chinese mythology and is sometimes likened to the roc. Its story is derived from the Taoist classic Zhuangzi (莊子). The "journey of the peng" means a long, promising future.

46 This poem as well as much of Tang poetry incorporate references to famed historical personages, linking the present world with past glories. This poetic technique both serves to lend gravitas to the subject at hand, but also serves to inspire by citing national "heroes" as exemplars. In this case, it is a shorthand metaphor to illustrate the difficulties of waiting for a petition to be approved. See Names and Terms, "Li Guang."

48.1 "Doumen": an area southwest of the Pearl River Delta, was once part of Heungshan County but now forms a separate district within Zhuhai, a prefecture level city bordering Macau.

"Tahiti": the poem makes reference to a place named 大溪地 or "daaih kaih deih" (big creek ground), the identification of which is a bit uncertain due to the various informal place names used by early Chinese immigrants. However, this term is also the name for the French Overseas Collectivity of Tahiti where Chinese immigrants first arrived in 1865 to work in cotton plantations. It is not known how many might have traveled between Tahiti and California. These sojourners were of Hakka and Punti heritage, and their descendants remain part of Tahitian society today.

51 This poem is signed by Lum as the "Taoist of Tit Sèhng." He laments his fate as an Angel Island detainee in a 4-character, 10-line regulated verse. A companion poem was written by another and is included as Poem 52 below.

52 A companion to Poem 51, this poem is an example of artistic plundering where its writer adds one opening character to each line of the first poem, then adds two extra lines for a different conclusion at the end. The poem is now different, employing a 1st person plural voice to replace the earlier's 1st person singular. How much time elapsed between the two poems or whether the authors knew each other is unknown. And to think that this poetic exchange may have taken place over days, months, or even years!

52.12 "swear to cut off the barbarians' heads": is a figurative expression of the detainee poet's anger and frustration. China with its 4,000 year old history of dynasties has certainly had its share of wars and violent conflict creating a store of associated imagery. Other Angel Island literary references include exploding bombs and eviscerated hearts and guts. Despite the anger and rage expressed in this work, no records of violence perpetrated by detainees against officials exist. Detainees were careful not to jeopardize their ultimate goal of a successful landing.

To address grievances, promote well-being and resolve interpersonal conflicts, detainees organized 自治會 or "zih chih wui" ("self-governing associations"). These associations were instrumental in negotiating with officials to improve food quality due to insufficient funding and poor judgment by institutional procurers.

On the other hand, detainees were aware of the potential for violence against them in the history of anti-Chinese incidents in the latter 19th century, most famous of which was the Rock Springs Massacre which occurred on September 2, 1885 in Wyoming, where 28 Chinese miners were brutally murdered. No indictments were ever returned nor charges filed in this incident. Reparations were paid by the federal government only for property loss.

53 A fine example of the use of historical allusion in classical Chinese poetry, the "imitate exemplary heroes" motif. In its eight lines this poem lists at least five cultural references, an accretion of detail which lends power to the poem's petitioning question.

Without a native knowledge of Chinese history and culture, the specific import of each incident may not be easily grasped. An equivalent American historical allusion might be to the story of George Washington and the cherry tree where the idea of honesty is implied in the narrative. The See Names and Terms section includes some for additional information on historical figures mentioned here: Wu Zi, Master Su Qing, Jiyun, and Goujian.

54.2-3 "cut from the timber of Chu": during the Spring and Autumn Period (770-476 BCE), natural resources were taken from the state of Chu and used by the state of Jin, symbolizing native materials exploited for use in a foreign land.

54.10 "Loulan": a state during the Western Han dynasty (206 BCE-24 CE), it is presently located in Xinjiang province. In 77 BCE, the Han emperor ordered the assassination of the Loulan king who was unfriendly towards the Chinese.

57 The first character of each vertical line in the Chinese text read across from right to left makes up the phrase 埃崙待劇 or "Island awaits leveling," making this an acrostic-like poem. The English translation tries to incorporate this formal feature.

58 This response to Poem 57 uses the same end-rhyme words in Chinese. Artistically it's another example of poetic collaboration, and politically of mutual support among detainees where the wall poetry helped establish a sense of community.

58.2 "Confucius": while in exile, Confucius and his disciples were on the road between the kingdoms of Chen and Cai, and some feared his appointment in the powerful neighboring state of Chu. He was placed under house arrest and troops were ordered to surround them, falling in danger of famine.

59 Chinese mythological figures are used here to highlight the powerlessness of the detainees. Of note is that this poem was carved backwards onto the men's barrack walls. In the State of California-sponsored study, *Poetry and Inscriptions: Translation and Analysis Angel Island Immigration Station*, the authors describe the poem thusly:

> "A poem that was carved backwards, or in reverse, such as when one is preparing to print on a printing press. This gives rise to the idea that the carvers of the poetry were not necessarily the authors of the poems. The carver of this particular piece may not have been literate, or may have been a carver of wood block prints who inadvertently carved this poem backwards (Island Poem 42, Photo 47447, Location 205-E-3). It could also have been deliberately carved backwards so that other immigrants could make rubbings as souvenirs."

This "backwards carving" is also consistent with the poem's theme of reversal of fortune and re-empowerment where "wronged" things are made right again. Assuming that the reverse calligraphy was intentional, it's a marvelous example of conceptual art where form is also part of meaning. Because of the complex semiotics of Chinese characters (see

Pound and Fennelosa), Chinese poetry has always had a visual aspect, from its sheer calligraphic beauty to the traditional pairing of verse with watercolor painting, for example in the work of Wang Wei.

60.2 "Because of the mouth": means to feed oneself, to make a living.

60.7 "What's more, must stand naked, just to check the lungs": refers to the detainees' shame in having to expose their bodies to doctors during the health exams, which was contrary to Chinese cultural norms of physical modesty.

60.11 In Chinese, the character for heart 心 or "sam" can also mean spirit and the metaphor of intestines or guts evokes internal fortitude.

61.1 During the exclusion era, many Chinese illegally entered the United States through Mexico.

61.6-7 See Names and Terms, "Ruan Ji" and "Li Ling."

62.8 "jingwei bird": the 精衛 is a bird in Chinese mythology, who was transformed from Yandi's daughter. While playing in the Eastern Sea, she drowned and changed into a bird called the "Jingwei," which carried pebbles or twigs from the Western Mountains in its beak and dropped them into the sea hoping to fill it. From this myth comes the Chinese idiom 精卫填海 or "Jingwei Tries to Fill the Sea" meaning dogged determination and perseverance in face of impossible odds. Here the meaning is rather ironic expressing the futility of human endeavors.

63.9 The romanization of Chinese surnames such as 許 or "Hui" follows spelling conventions for Cantonese immigrants based upon area of origin. Thus popular surnames use different English spellings depending upon the pronunciation in different dialects. For example, the surname 林 or "Lin" in Hanyu Pinyin is also romanized as "Lam" (Sam Yahp or Guangzhou dialects), "Lum" (Heungshan dialect), and "Lim" (Sze Yap or Toishan dialects). When district origin is clearly indicated, surnames are dialect specific.

65.6 A footnote in *Island* references "the wild wave" from a quotation in an essay by Han Yu, a scholar and official during the Tang dynasty (618-907 CE). It states that "to return the violent wave that had fallen," is to make an effort to restore declined fortunes.

67.5 "Napoleon": this political leader was imprisoned in 1814 on the island of Elba but subsequently escaped to regain power in France. He was deposed after his eventual demise at the Battle of Waterloo in 1815.

69 Another fragment poem, this one is missing sixteen characters from the beginnings of each line, yet some information can be inferred from the rest of the text. Most likely planks that included the missing carved text had been destroyed and replaced.

69.4 The missing characters are likely the name of Confucius who was once surrounded for seven days.

69.8 The missing characters here probably relate to taming the "monkey mind" in order to achieve grace and simplicity.

NAMES AND TERMS

Persons

Confucius (551-479 BCE) was a Chinese teacher, editor, politician, and philosopher of the Spring and Autumn period of Chinese history. Confucius' family name was Kong Qiu (孔丘 or Kǒng Qiū), and he is also known by the honorific Kong Fuzi (孔夫子 or Kǒng Fūzǐ, literally "Grand Master Kong"). The philosophy of Confucius emphasized personal and governmental morality, correctness of social relationships, justice and sincerity. Confucius is traditionally credited with having authored or edited many of the Chinese classic texts including all of the Five Classics.

Goujian was the king of the state of Yue. In 493 BCE, he was shamefully defeated by King Fuchai's armies from the state of Wu. Two decades later in 473 BCE, Yue recovered and returned to defeat Wu, whose territory was annexed to Goujian's territories. While recovering from his first defeat, Goujian ate food suited for peasants, as well as forcing himself to taste bile, in order to remember his humiliations while serving under the State of Wu. The Chinese idiom 臥薪嘗膽 or "sleeping on sticks and tasting gall," refers to Goujian's perseverance.

Li Guang (?-119 BCE) nicknamed "Flying General" by the Xiongnu was a general serving Emperor Wu of the Western Han dynasty. Despite being a tough opponent, he was never conferred a noble title. He was haunted by what some scholars characterized as "bad luck." Li Guang was a descendant of Lao Tze, and Li Ling was his grandson.

Li Ling (?-74 BCE), a Han general, led an army of foot soldiers against the Xiongnu. After fighting against great odds, he was forced to surrender and defected to the Xiongnu. The Han emperor subsequently executed his family, while Li Ling never returned to the Han.

Nan Jiyun (?-757 CE). During the An Lushan rebellion against the Tang army (755-760 CE), the rebels surrounded Suiyang. Nan was one of the defenders of the besieged city, a soldier captain, and shot the enemy general Yin Ziqi in the left eye with one arrow, providing a temporary victory for the Tang troops.

Ruan Ji (210-263 CE), a poet, musician and scholar during the period of the Three Kingdoms (220-280 CE), was a person who enjoyed drinking and visiting mountains and streams. It was said he often wandered in the hills and came back crying bitterly like a madman.

Su Qin (380-284 BCE), a scholar during the Warring States period (475-221 BCE), was unsuccessful in gaining an official post after finishing his studies. Returning home, he was driven to study harder by stabbing himself in the thigh with a sharp instrument, epitomizing extreme diligence and concentrated effort See Note 2.2.

Su Wu (140-60 BCE), also known as Su Qing, was sent by the Chinese government during the Western Han dynasty (206 BCE-24 CE), as a diplomat to Xiongnu, the kingdom of nomadic people north of China. Su Wu was detained there for 19 years but remained loyal to the Han emperor. Su is regarded as an example of great faith and courage performed by officials.

Wu Yun (?-484 BCE) or Wu Zixu was the son of a high official serving King Ping of Chu. His father fell into the king's disfavor and was killed together with his family. Wu Zixu, however, fled to the state of Wu. Later, Wu Zixu became an important official serving the Wu king and led an army to defeat the state of Chu. As the Wu army entered the Chu capital in 506 B.C., Wu Zixu dug up the corpse of King Ping and whipped it 300 times.

Places
"Aai Leuhn" (埃崙) is a transliteration of the name "Angel Island" and was a colloquial designation used by the Cantonese immigrants.

Gold Mountain or "Gām Sàan" (金山) is a colloquial Chinese name for California See Note 4.4.

Heungshan County (香山) is located on the west side of the Pearl River Delta across from Hong Kong and Shenzen. It was renamed Chungshan County (中山) in 1928 to honor Dr. Sun Yat-sen, considered to be the "Father of Modern China" by both the People's Republic of China and the Republic of China. Today its romanized name is Zhongshan, and it is a prefecture-level city encompassing both county and township levels of government.

"Tang Mountain" or "Tohng Saan" (唐山) is another Cantonese colloquialism for China. The Cantonese consider themselves descendants of the Tang people who ruled during the Tang dynasty.

Toishan County (台山), located southwest of the Pearl River Delta, is part of a geographical area originally known as Sze Yap (Four Counties) including Toisan, Sunwui, Hoiping, and Yanping. The largest percentage of Chinese immigrants to the U.S. and Canada call these counties their ancestral home.

Wood house (木屋) or "muhk uhk" was a popular term for the Immigration Station's men's barracks. With its Douglas Fir construction, it is the main site for the wall inscriptions. See Notes 7.9 and 15.1 for reference.

Terms
Barbarians/foreign slaves or "faan nouh" (番奴) refers to non-Han Chinese invaders who at various times ruled China. It is also a derogatory term for Westerners.

Chang'e (嫦娥) is the Chinese goddess of the moon. The story of Chang'e relates to the origin of the Mid-Autumn Moon Festival. In a far distant past, ten suns rose together into the skies and scorched the earth, bringing hardship to the people. The archer Hou Yi shot down nine, leaving just one sun, and was given the elixir of immortality as a reward. He did not drink it right away, but hid it at home, thinking that he did not want to gain immortality without his beloved wife Chang'e. However while Yi was out hunting, Pengmeng broke into his house and tried to force Chang'e to give him the elixir; she refused and drank it herself. Chang'e then flew upwards towards the heavens. Her great love for her husband drew her towards the Moon, which is the nearest celestial body to the earth. Hou Yi, discovering what had happened and feeling great sadness, displayed the fruits and cakes that Chang'e had liked and gave sacrifices to her.

Foreign devils," 番鬼 or "faan gwai" ("foreign devils") and 鬼佬 or "gwai lou" ("devil person") were vernacular Cantonese terms for white people who ironically were seen as "foreigners" even though it was the Chinese who were migrating to America to live and work.

Jingwei bird (精衛) is a bird in Chinese mythology who was transformed from Yandi's daughter. See Note 62.8.

Mid-Autumn Festival, this annual event occurs on the 15th day of the 9th month in the lunar calendar and marks the celebration of the Fall harvest.

Qiqiao Festival or the "Seventh Day of the Seventh Moon" is a cultural event celebrated among Chinese. As legend has it, the Weaver Girl (Zhinu) came down from heaven one day and fell in love with a mortal Cowherd (Niulang). After their marriage, her loom which once wove colorful clouds fell silent. Angered, the Goddess of Heaven ordered her back to work and separated the two by placing Zhinu and Niulang in different constellations with the Milky Way in between. Each year, they are allowed to meet on the seventh day of the seventh moon, when magpies fly up into the heavens to form a bridge.

Terrace for Gazing Homeward (望鄉臺) or "mohng heung toih" ("gaze village platform") is a place where one could ascend to gaze in the direction of his or her former home. See Note 44.7.

Terrace of Yang (陽台) or "yeuhng toih" ("male platform") derives from Song Yu's "Rhapsody on the High Terrace" where King Huai of Chu (328-299 BCE) met the spirit of Shamanka Mountain in a dream and had sexual relations with her. In bidding him goodbye, she said "I live on the sunny side of Shamanka Mountain, at the dangerous point of the highest hill. At sunrise I am the morning clouds and at sunset, the traveling rains. Morning after morning, sunset after sunset, I am below the Yang Terrace." The expression "clouds and rain" denoting romance and the act of physical love, comes from this story.

INDEX OF FIRST LINES AND TITLES

Following the first lines of the poems are poem numbers. Poems which were given actual titles have been bolded.

When I left, my parents regretted the hurry, 5
Whereas, my countryman, the family was split up to advance, 3
Young children don't yet know worry, 34
[   ] male eagle also easy to tame, 69

FURTHER READING

Barnstone, Tony, and Chou Ping, editors. *The Anchor Book of Chinese Poetry*. Translated by Tony Barnstone and Chou Ping, Anchor, 2004.

Biguenet, John, and Rainier Schulte, editors. *The Craft of Translation*. University of Chicago Press, 1989

Cai, Zong-Qi, editor. *How to Read Chinese Poetry: a Guided Anthology*. Columbia University Press, 2008.

Chang, Iris. *The Chinese in America: A Narrative History*. Viking, 2003.

Heng-t'ang-t'ui-shih, editor. *The Jade Mountain: A Chinese Anthology, Being Three Hundred Poems of the Tang Dynasty, 618-906*. Translated by Witter Bynner and Kiang Kang-Hu, Alfred A. Knopf, 1929.

Heng-t'ang-t'ui-shih, editor. *The Three Hundred Tang Poems*. Translated by Innes Herdan, Far East Book Company, 1973.

Hinton, David, editor. *Classical Chinese Poetry: An Anthology*. Translated by David Hinton, Farrar Strauss Giroux, 2008.

Hom, Marlon K. *Songs of Gold Mountain: Cantonese Rhymes from San Francisco Chinatown*. Translated by Marlon K. Hom, University of California Press, 1987.

Huang, Yunte. *Transpacific Imaginations: History, Literature, Counterpoetics*. Harvard University Press, 2008.

Lai, Him Mark, Genny Lim, and Judy Yung, editors. *Island: Poetry and History of Chinese Immigrants on Angel Island 1910-1940* 2nd edition, translated by Him Mark Lai and Genny Lim, University of Washington Press, 2014.

Lee, Erika. *The Making of Asian America: A History*. Simon & Schuster, 2015.

Lee, Erika and Judy Yung. *Angel Island: Immigrant Gateway to America*. Oxford University Press, 2010.

Liu, Wan. "Analysis of the Poems Inscribed or Composed at the Angel Island Immigration Station." *Poetry and Inscriptions: Translation and Analysis*. Architectural Resources Group, 2004.

Liu, Yuxi. "Loushi Ming (Inscription about a Crude Dwelling)." *The Feng Shui Architect's Blog*. Translated by Howard Choy, 20 March 2013, howardchoy.wordpress.com/2013/03/20/loushi-ming-inscription-about-a-crude-dwelling.

Merwin, William Stanley, translator. *East Window: The Asian Translations*. Copper Canyon Press, 2009.

Pound, Ezra. *Cathay: Translations by Ezra Pound for the Most Part from the Chinese of Rihaku, from the Notes of the Late Ernest Fenollosa, and the Decipherings of the Professors Mori and Ariga* Elkin Matthews, Cork Street, 1915.

Pound, Ezra and Ernest Fenollosa. *Instigations of Ezra Pound Together with an Essay on the Chinese Written Character by Ernest Fenollosa*. Boni and Liveright, 1920

Rexroth, Kenneth, translator. *One Hundred Poems from the Chinese*. New Directions, 1971.

Schulte, Rainer, and John Biguenet, editors. *Theories of Translation*. University of Chicago Press, 1992.

Seidensticker, Edward. "On Trying to Translate Japanese." *Encounter*, August, 1958, pp. 12-19.

Shinn, Christopher A. "Between Walls: So Much Depends Upon Chinese Immigrant Poetry in Defining the Modernist Age." *American Modernist Poetry and the Chinese Encounter*. Edited by Zhang Yuejun and Stuart Christie, Palgrave/MacMillan, 2012, pp. 19-47.

Snyder, Gary. *Riprap and Cold Mountain Poems*. Counterpoint, 1965.

Stewart, Frank, editor. *The Poem Behind the Poem*. Copper Canyon Press, 2004.

Sze, Arthur. *The Redshifting Web: Poems 1970-1998*. Copper Canyon Press, 1998.

Teow Lim Goh. *Islanders*. Conundrum Press, 2016.

Waley, Arthur. *The Poet Li Po, A.D. 701-762*. China Society, School of Oriental Studies, London: East and West, Ltd., 1919.

Williams, R. John. "Decolonizing Cathay: Teaching the Scandals of Translation through Angel Island Poetry." *Transformations*, vol. XVII, no.2, Fall 2006-Winter 2007, pp. 15-30.

Wright, James. *Collected Poems*. Wesleyan University Press, 1971.

Yang, Liping. *Translation, Rewriting, and the Modernization of China*. Dissertation, National University of Singapore, 2006.

Yao, Stephen G. "Transplantation and Modernity: The Chinese/American Poems of Angel Island." *Sinographies: Writing China*. Edited by Eric Hayot, Haun Saussy, and Steven G. Yao. University of Minnesota Press, 2008.

Yep, Laurence with Dr. Kathleen S. Yep. *The Dragon's Child: A Story of Angel Island*. Harper, 2008.

Yip, Wai-Lim. *Chinese Poetry: An Anthology of Major Modes and Genres*. Translated by Wai-Lim Yip, Duke University Press, 1997.

--- *Ezra Pound's "Cathay"*. Princeton University Press, 1969.

Young, David, translator. *Du Fu: A Life in Poetry*. Alfred A. Knopf, 2015.

ACKNOWLEDGMENTS

In November 2016 I traveled with my wife and daughter to visit for the first time my parents' ancestral villages in Guangdong Province, China. There I photographed on a white-washed living room wall in the house where my mother was born, two framed documents with ink-brushed Chinese characters detailing my maternal genealogy back some 26 generations, perhaps up to 500 years past. This formal record would end with my grandparents immigrating to the United States in the early 20th century.

Here in a new Millennium, descendants of villagers welcomed us as returning "Wah Kue" or overseas Chinese. Suddenly I realized that it has taken this village and many others, a vast network of peoples and places, to create the person I am today, both as individual and as a writer. For this, I am forever grateful and humbled.

And in a similar sense, it has taken a great village to spawn the translations in this book. The largest debt of course is to those anonymous detainees at the Angel Island Immigration Station who felt compelled to carve their words, their souls no less, into the Douglas Fir plank walls of the men's barracks. This book in essence will always be theirs.

But the fact of preservation of this literary work owes as much to Smiley Jann and Tet Yee, fellow detainees who had the foresight to copy characters off the walls into notebooks. And much is owed to the Chinatown community activists who in the late 1970s saved the Immigration Station men's barracks from demolition.

A huge debt is owed to Him Mark Lai and Genny Lim, two co-authors of *Island: Poetry and History of Chinese Immigrants on Angel Island 1910-1940*, self-published in 1980, which offered the first English translations of the wall poems. Co-author Judy Yung added invaluable oral history interviews of Angel Island detainees to that book. The American public's general awareness of the Angel Island experience has been largely due to the efforts of these three writers. In particular Judy Yung has been extraordinarily kind to me, making available copies of *Island*'s English and Chinese texts when, as a graduate student, I first grappled with translation.

And further thank yous to Ben K. Lee and Ben Fenkell for facilitating an extraordinary day of photography at the Angel Island Immigration Station.

On a more personal level, I am grateful for my past poetry teacher-mentors: Julie Bruck, and at the Vermont College of Fine Arts MFA in Writing Program, Natasha Sajé, Betsy Sholl, Richard Jackson, and David Wojahn, all who encouraged me in retranslating this work. I thank my extraordinary VCFA classmates too, especially Ann Huang and Dave Celone for their support of translation, and to the San Leandro Public Library staff, Addie Silveira and Mary Beth Barloga, more thank yous.

Some of these Chinese translations first appeared online in *Eleven Eleven Literary Review* and *Poetry Flash*. A few of my original poems about the Angel Island experience were also published in *Bamboo Ridge* and *Crab Orchard Review*. And I can never express enough thanks to Calypso Editions and my editor Martin Woodside for their unparalleled literary vision and unwavering support for this project.

Lastly, no appreciation will be complete without acknowledgment of my own personal village, my father and mother who taught me the Zhongshan dialect of Cantonese as a child and, most importantly, explicated to my sister and me around the dinner table nuances of an immigrant culture that are at the heart of these poems. They are my first family.

And today as my family expands, much gratitude is given to my wife Lauren and daughter Mari with their own immigrant-related stories and writings, particularly to my daughter who as a preteen started me on this journey, displaying a Chinese character drawn on her handheld device while visiting Angel Island a few summers ago. They are at the center of my village, which expands again in every reader who finds in these pages a love of social justice and poetry.

ABOUT THE TRANSLATOR

Jeffrey Thomas Leong is a poet and writer, born in Southern California and raised in the San Francisco Bay Area. He holds an MFA degree from the Vermont College of Fine Arts, and a BA and JD from the University of California at Berkeley, where he helped found the Asian American Studies program in the 1970s. For over twenty years he worked as a public health administrator and attorney for the City of San Francisco.

His writing has appeared in *Crab Orchard Review, Cimarron Review, Bamboo Ridge, Hyphen, Cha: A Literary Journal, Spillway, Eleven Eleven Literary Journal, Poetry Flash,* and elsewhere. He lives with his wife and daughter in the East Bay. *www.jeffreythomasleong.com*

ABOUT THE PUBLISHER

Calypso Editions is a cooperative, artist-run, 501(c)(3) non-profit press dedicated to publishing quality literary books of poetry and fiction with a global perspective.

We believe that literature is essential to building an international community of readers and writers and that, in a world of digital saturation, books can serve as physical artifacts of beauty and wonder.

CALYPSO EDITIONS

info@CalypsoEditions.org | www.CalypsoEditions.org

Original Poetry

CALYPSO EDITIONS

www.CalypsoEditions.org

Blue Structure
by Jan Freeman
Poetry

*While Everything Slipped Away
From Me*
by Erika Lutzner
Poetry

*City that Ripens on the
Tree of the World*
by Robin Davidson
Poetry

Use
by Derick Burleson
Poetry

Contemporary Poetry in Translation
CALYPSO EDITIONS
www.CalypsoEditions.org

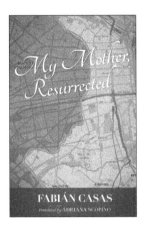

My Mother, Resurrected
by Fabián Casas
Translated by Adriana Scopino
Poetry

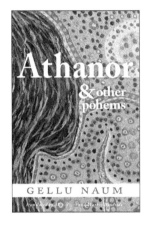

Athanor and Other Pohems
by Gellu Naum
Translated by Margento and
Martin Woodside
Poetry

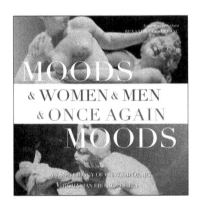

*Moods & Women & Men & Once Again
Moods: An Anthology of Contemporary
Romanian Erotic Poetry*
Edited by Ruxandra Cesereanu
Poetry

Stomach of the Soul
by Sylva Fischerová
Tranlated by the author,
with Stuart Friebert
and A. J. Hauner
Poetry

Original Fiction
CALYPSO EDITIONS
www.CalypsoEditions.org

The Little Trilogy
by Anton Chekhov
Translated by Boris Dralyuk
Fiction

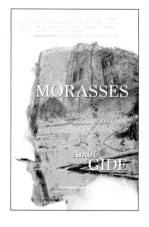

Morasses
by André Gide
Translated by Tadzio Koelb
Fiction

Ilona. My Life with the Bard
by Jana Juráňová
Translated by Julia
and Peter Sherwood
Fiction

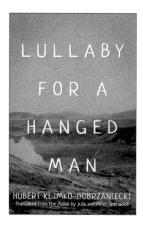

Lullaby For a Hanged Man
by Hubert Klimko-Dobrzaniecki
Translated by Julia and Peter Sherwood
Fiction